Only By Grace

A Candid Look
at the Life of a Minister

by Tom S. Sampson

CBP Press
St. Louis, Missouri

Unless otherwise indicated, all scripture quotations are from the Revised Standard Version of the Bible, copyrighted 1946, 1952, © 1971, 1973, by the Division of Christian Education of the National Council of the Churches of Christ in the United States of America, and used by permission.

Library of Congress Cataloging in Publication Data

Sampson, Tom S.
    Only by grace.

    1. Clergy—Religious life. 2. Clergy—Psychology. 3. Pastoral theology. 4. Sampson, Tom. S.
I. Title.
BV4011.6.S25   1986   248.8'92   85-29916
ISBN 0-8272-2707-8

Printed in the United States of America

Dedication

To my peers in ministry and friends in several parishes who are moved by the Spirit and have concern for the poor, I dedicate this book.

Their faithful examples have deepened my commitment to God and given purpose to my life through the fellowship we have shared in the name of Jesus Christ.

The proceeds from this book are pledged to the education of women and minority men preparing for ministry.

Contents

Introduction

More books have been written about Jesus Christ than anyone else in history. Few books, however, explain the inner lives of the ministers who preach about him.

There are more commentaries on the Bible than any other book. Yet few authors interpret the inner struggles of pastors who rely on the scriptures.

Thousands of words interpret theological viewpoints, but relatively few describe the personal lifestyles of the ministers who live by those theologies.

This book introduces the spiritual issues which shape pastors' daily ministry. It focuses on one clergyperson in particular but speaks in general about the men and women who preach the word, administer the sacraments, serve the church, and love the Lord.

. . . .

Any detailed account of a minister's life and job reveals what a complex pilgrimage it can be to follow the Master.

God deals with each of us in ways to fit our individual lives. Any suggestion that one book could explain ministry is arrogant. This book deals only with the spiritual choices ministers face in their daily work.

Writing such a book is dangerous.

It is dangerous because I write concerning a topic with which thousands of clergy are already very familiar. I am under no illusion that a great many could write a better book about ministers than I. But few undertake such an introduction. I must count on the patience and forebearance of those more capable than I to add to my true observations and forgive my false conclusions.

. . . .

Two explanations about the construction of this book:

One: I have used phrases of the Lord's Prayer only as chapter headings. They help focus on the salient aspects of ministry. "Thy Will Be Done" suggests the practical side of the pastor's work;

while "Forgive Us Our Sins" points to problems in which clergy, like all human beings, often become involved.

Two: I have tried to deal with every major part of the clergy's personal and public life which is affected by his or her spiritual decisions. Each area is introduced by an editorial essay. This has been followed by an example taken from real-life experiences. Thus, faith and works balance each other as they always should.

. . . .

I want to explain that this is not a book about how the church can change the world. That in itself is extremely important and I admire many of my peers who should write (and have written) significant accounts of their extraordinary ministries. In particular, I respect the pastors who do exceptional work in inner city churches of the poor, I revere my pastor friends who are on the frontier of social change and whose churches have become sanctuaries for the afflicted. And I hold in high regard my peers who, as women clergy, are leading the church in Christlike new directions. However, this book is not an exciting report on such significant ministries. I must leave those important accomplishments in more capable hands. Instead, this volume is a description of the personal, spiritual battles which take place in pastor's lives behind the work they do. This book is not how pastors change others, but rather how they, with the help of God, change themselves.

. . . .

Only By Grace is written with the hope of helping more people understand the role of the pastor.

For there are those who are unacquainted with what the clergyperson is like. Some see the pastor as out of touch with the world and living in a fool's paradise of peace and love. Others see the pastor on an unapproachable pedestal. Many conclude the pastor has a "hot- line" to God, which enables him or her to cure all ills and even manage the weather. Any number of people see their minister as living in another world, far from the tough decisions that confront persons in everyday life.

The facts are that the clergy are combinations of worldly sophistication and heavenly vision. We deal in human sin, but we have an eye on forgiveness and on triumph over evil. We have warts as well as halos. None of us is perfect. We have human doubt, but we also have an awareness of the presence of God. Each of us is on a spiritual journey that often frustrates us but that rewards us with a hope and a vision of what the world will someday be like.

Having said this, we must also note that there are parts of the pastor's life that are probably unknown, especially to laypersons. Indeed, not all of us know the intricacies of faith and belief that motivate and sustain the man or woman who conducts worship for us in our church. Few of us are aware of how our minister may struggle with spiritual and personal problems connected with being a clergyperson. How many of us understand the failures as well as the great victories of faith that our pastors experience in their discipleship with our Lord?

For those who are looking for a candid, open, and confessional introduction to the life of a pastor, *Only By Grace* is an answer.

Our Father
Who Art
in Heaven

Could we with ink the oceans fill,
    And were the heavens of parchment made,
Were every talk on earth a quill
    and every man a scribe by trade,
To write the love of God above
    Would drain the ocean dry,
Nor could the scroll contain the whole
    Though stretched from sky to sky."
                —*Chaldee Ode* sung in Jewish synagogues
                on the first day of the feast of Pentecost.

My Fur-Lined Gloves

A man I never met, whose name I will never know, became a guide and companion on my journey toward God.

I saw him unexpectedly on a very chilly day. I had just left a hospital where I had visited a friend. I was challenging the cutting wind as I walked to my car, when I saw this man approaching on the snowy sidewalk. He, too, was struggling against the bitter cold. As he leaned into the wind, he kept trying with one hand to keep his skimpy overcoat closed. He kept the other hand as warm as possible in a pocket. He wore no boots, even though there were drifts almost everywhere.

As we approached each other, I thought of the differences in our lives. I was warm in a well-lined overcoat, while he could scarcely keep out the cold. I was from an affluent suburban life, while he appeared to be part of a poverty-stricken ghetto only blocks away. I was "privileged American." He was "poor Spanish."

But it was not just the obvious differences that have stuck in my memory. It was what happened when he and I passed each other. Conflicting feelings unsettled me.

Who was I to be clothed in comfort while he lacked warm clothing? Was it really fair that I had so much in life while he had so little? Was I not expected, in my role as minister, to share with the "least" and call them brothers?

Suddenly I had a tremendous urge to yank off my fur-lined gloves and press them into his bare hands.

By the time this thought had gone through my mind, the man had passed by.

Should I run after him and call, "Here, friend, take these; I want to share what I have with you"?

But I did not. I was afraid. What would he think? Would his pride keep him from even answering me? Was it right for me to invade his poverty? Would he look upon me as offering charity? Would he understand my Christian effort to be a brother?

Unfortunately, he was now down the street beyond hearing my voice.

So, I never gave my gloves to that frost-bitten man. I have often wished I had, for that brief encounter has become a symbol of my growth as a person.

That man has become all of humanity to me. His struggle in such flimsy clothes against the cold of winter, and my warmth in winter overcoat and gloves, symbolize the gulf between those who "have" and those who "have not."

He was so much like me. He, too, must have known the threat of winter and the passion for warmth. He, too, must have wanted a secure home and friends who would take him in. He, too, must have cried when life became bitter and must have loved

10

when he could. How really alike we both were, how much a part of each other, brothers in the struggle for life!

But I rejected the human bonds that made us brothers.

Why did I have the gloves and not he? Was it luck or reason? And could it be justified? We had both started off, as babies, with the hope of a full life within our hearts. Was it fate that placed me in a home which was economically secure in contrast to his? Was it luck that I had a guaranteed future because I was white American and that he was denied his rightful opportunities just because he belonged to a minority? If it was a matter of my luck and not his, then I was obliged to share what I had not earned.

Or did I deserve my security and my position? Perhaps so, or perhaps not. If struggle produces character (as the apostle Paul suggests), then the stranger may have had more character than I. Comparative riches had come to me; he had to fight for every bit he got. Had it given him perseverance? Had he learned the necessity of hope? Had he accepted the promises of God to those who put their faith in God and not in things, as I had done? No, God is good to all of us, whether we deserve it or not. Sometimes God is even more loving when we do not deserve it (in order to prove how much God loves us). So, I should have shared with that man, whether he deserved it or not.

What chords of response did that man call forth from me? Why didn't I just bury my face in my coat and pass him by without further thought? Why does he continue to speak to me? Was it because we were so close and yet so different? If so, is that a clue to helping the rich share with the poor—by confronting them with the obviousness of poverty and oppression, by breaking down the walls by which those who "have" insulate themselves from knowing about those who "have not"?

Was there something in my very nature which made me responsive to that shivering man? Was it my interest in people and in ministering to them that affected me? Are people who love people and want to serve them more sensitive to life than those who spend their days making money and living in big houses? Are there rewards to caring for those in need which the wealthy know nothing about?

Finally, this staggering thought, what if that man was Christ?

The Gospel-writer Matthew tells of persons who met Christ and wondered why he said they had met him before. "It was when I was naked and you clothed me," he explained. But they replied, "When did we see you naked and clothed you?" Jesus answered, "As you did it unto the least of these, my brethren, you did it unto me" (Matt. 25:39).

Did I pass by Jesus? Whether I passed by him or not, my commitment to human brotherhood found me lacking. Now I cannot forget the incident. The lesson remains with me. The call continues to expect a response.

Answering the call has proven to be an eventful pilgrimage. Like many of the disciples, I have been both unfaithful and faithful. Like Peter, I have both denied my Lord and loved him. Like many of my peers in ministry, I have had moments of defeat and times of victory. I have been both cold and hot. I have known both doubt and miracles. But whatever the circumstances, I have never regretted answering the call of Christ.

Answering the Call of God

I grew up in a nonchurch home. Although my parents were both moral people, they never took an interest in the church. In fact, my only introduction to the church was when a childhood friend took me to his Episcopal Sunday School for a visit. From then until I left college, I saw no need for religion. After all, I was young. I knew what the world was all about. I could take care of myself. I had no need of God, even if God existed. Besides, I was afraid that if I took an interest in religious things in high school I would be called a "Christer," and I certainly could not stand that loss of standing among my peers.

After graduating from college, I obtained a job in a brokerage house, dealing in stocks and bonds. Was not the purpose of life to make money? However, I soon observed that many people with money did not really seem to be any happier than those without. Their lives and faces often revealed an anxiety about life that made me uncomfortable. I felt that some of those wealthy people were unreal, that they put too much emphasis upon things and position. So I reconsidered my association with the money markets.

12

My second breakthrough into maturity was prompted by the fact that I was working in a strange city, far away from old friends. I was lonely, especially on weekends. The only place I could find open was a church, so I began to attend Sunday services out of boredom, as well as curiosity about anything new. There I heard sermons that challenged my youthful conceit. I finally began to admit that there was something greater in life than myself.

But I was not ready for the church then. I knew I wanted to help people, but I did not know how. I wondered about becoming a social worker. I felt that kind of a job would allow me to help individuals or families adjust to financial or personal crises. But how could I afford my new interest? I had no money! So I began work as a door-to-door book salesman and at the same time arranged to attend a school of social work.

This plan quickly changed when an influential friend suggested that, instead of selling books I could work in a neighborhood house, a center for social and religious activities in an ethnic part of the city. I would be a recreational director on weekdays and serve a small congregation of only twenty people on Sundays as its pastor. I could attend social work classes at other times.

With the optimism and energy of youth, I began all three projects. Youth does not realize the subtle ways its innate talents can shape the future. Soon I found that the religious work with young people and their parents was more interesting than either life as a recreational director or employment as a social worker.

I felt social work might help people make important decisions, but such choices seemed to me to be relatively temporary and possibly superficial. The problems of meeting financial crises, getting jobs, or how to care for ailing relatives are certainly significant concerns, but I felt there were even deeper matters of life including the right goals and reasons for living, and the very will and courage to go on. More and more I turned my attention toward the church, which I thought spoke to these more fundamental concerns. After a few months I dropped out of social work school and enrolled in a seminary.

I wanted to be a minister because it seemed to me to be the most reasonable life to live. Religious objectives such as peace, equality of opportunity for all people, justice tempered with mercy—all these seemed to me to be just plain good sense. It was not even a matter of believing in God. Reason dictated to me that the church and religion stood for the best things in life. If God could be added so much the better, but at that time, such a presence did not concern me.

It was not long before a very significant event occurred. I had been in religion classes and was finding leadership of the small congregation to be more and more satisfying when I was told by officials of the denomination: "You must obtain a license even to be a beginning student pastor. You will be interviewed concerning your character and beliefs."

After a few weeks I was called before a group of four clergymen. They inquired about my background, why I wanted to be a pastor, and what I believed.

"I believe the world is founded on order," I explained. "I believe the world is good. I believe the Bible is the best guide to morality and purpose. And I believe that Jesus was the greatest example of faith and works."

Other questions followed, then I was asked: "Do you believe in God?"

Without a moment of hesitation, because I was young and knew all the answers to everything, I replied: "No, I don't!"

After an unusually long silence, the chairman said, "That will be all. You may go."

I left the hearing room, assuming after brief reflection that the license would certainly be denied me. But it was not!

"We are granting you a temporary license," I was told, "because we believe that behind your uncertainty you really believe in God. We will speak with you again, however."

So I began my ministry on what I thought was my own reason. Now I know that those pastors understood me better than I knew myself. They saw through my youthful assurance.

The Various Calls of God

God calls in so many different ways. The youthful idealism of a high-schooler at a religious summer camp often starts young people thinking of ministry. Sometimes hero-worship of a home-town pastor turns youth toward the church.

14

Older men and women may turn to the pastorate in their middle years when they become disenchanted with the dishonesty, the unfair competition, and the greed they experience in their business careers.

Of course, there are those who follow their family traditions. They become pastors because they feel familiar with and want to carry on the work of their preacher father or preacher grandfather.

Still others enter the ministry as a result of a never-to-be-forgotten conversion experience. They "saw the Lord." They were miraculously healed. They received a message from God. They were saved when they thought all was lost. They found a new life in Christ.

Nor can we overlook those who become pastors because they want the prestige of the position, because they want the attention of being "the preacher," or because they have ego needs that must be met. They relish the dignity and influence of the clergy's role in a community.

But whatever our personal reasons for entering the pastorate, not one of us has chosen the church by ourselves. It is not our decision at all. We have responded to the irresistible call of our Creator.

It was not I who chose the church. It was God who chose me. Long before I was aware of my own personhood, the Spirit of Creation was calling me. I had within me a Spirit that was greater than my knowledge. It was not I who was really living, but the Spirit who was living within me.

At this point, a tremendous concern challenges me. Why should I be chosen to preach the gospel? Why, me, O Lord, when I know I am filled with so many imperfections? Why does God entrust the Word with me when my vessel is so weak?

There is no explanation as to why God chooses one person rather than another. In fact, God chooses all of us for something. I suspect God has different roles for each of us according to our individual talents. Some of us find ourselves to be pastors, others teachers, and some business people. The creativeness of God goes on in all sorts of ways to fashion a world which has all kinds of needs. God works through bankers, bricklayers, prophets, and apostles.

With the ever-increasing spread of knowledge, each type of work is a skill distinct unto itself. Each contributes to the whole.

The pastor can preach but he or she is dependent upon and learns from the trades of others!

Nor are any of us perfect. We are all imperfect to some degree, hence the importance of helping each other—yes, even praying for each other, which has often been the topic of my prayers. I as a pastor need to learn from the varying lives and works of those in my congregation.

As God uses me to speak to them, so God uses members of my parish to bring the Word to me.

A Prayer

I sit alone,
in my church office,
on Saturday night,
thinking about tomorrow.

The church will be bustling with activity.
Families and strangers will come for worship,
to hear the Word, and to share in living.

O Lord, look with grace upon the people!
Some are spiritually dead; help me awaken them.
Some are more intelligent than I; let me learn from them.
Some are too content; make me challenge them.
Some are more honest than I; help me to relate to them.
Some are threatened by circumstance;
        enable me to support them.
Some are more mature than I; open me to listen to them.
Some are satisfied through ignorance;
        let me disturb them.
Some are imprisoned by fear;
        empower me to release them.
Some are confused; help me to find clarity with them.
Some are so strong in their belief;
        let me celebrate with them.

                                        Amen.

Send Me . . . How, When, Where?

It was the prophet Isaiah in the Old Testament who heard the Voice saying, "Who will go for us?" Although he felt inadequate, he faithfully answered, "Here am I! Send me" (Isa. 6:8). In answering the call, every pastor faces similar questions, "What have I that the Lord needs? How is the Lord going to use my talents, even my weaknesses and my strengths? Where can I find the work that the Lord wants done?"

Direction is relatively easy for us. We have the Model! The purpose of our Lord's life must be ours!

> to preach goods news to the poor . . .
> to proclaim release to the captives . . .
> to set at liberty those who are oppressed. (Luke 4:18)

Still the question remains, *how* are we called to do these things?

Some of us discover we have the gift of preaching, some the faith to heal. There are those who understand the role of prophet-for-social-change, while others are equipped to instruct in the faith. Some have talents for evangelism, others travel to mission fields. Many serve in hospitals or prisons. Those of us who feel called to the parish ministry have a special role to play also. We must be with our parishioners in all sorts of circumstances. We visit them in their homes, we sit with them when they are hospitalized, we shed tears with them in times of sorrow, and may joyously celebrate with them on special occasions.

Walking in the shoes of our parishioners is our unique opportunity. It gives us the chance to find out how they live, to listen to their fears, to understand their doubts, to know their joys and to hear their problems.

One of the spiritual responsibilities of the parish minister is to preach to the concerns which directly affect people's lives. Unfortunately, in the beginning years of a pastor's career and sometimes even later, many pastors don't fulfill such a role. Because we have been academically trained, we tend to prolong this background; we have much book-learning but little experience, we have knowledge but not wisdom, we are acquainted with religious history but not with the spirit of the "street".

Of course, the best and possibly only remedy for this is more footwork and less headwork, more bell-pushing, more visiting, and more calling; all seasoned with a sincere interest in really hearing and carefully listening.

Just Listenin'

One day I had just finished my breakfast when I heard the distant siren of a fire engine. The sound became louder and nearer, then the engine turned onto my street and stopped nearby.

I grabbed my coat and rushed outside.

Down the block a house was on fire. I could see the firemen running into the place, pulling hoses behind them. Some were already smashing windows to let out dense black smoke. Smoldering furniture was thrown onto the lawn. Orders were shouted back and forth. The sidewalk filled with curious onlookers.

I did not know who lived in the house, but I wondered if it could be some poor people, a group of whom stood together on the lawn. They were new in our neighborhood.

I watched for some time until the fire seemed to be under control, and then I left. But I could not so easily leave my feelings. All day I wondered what the people were going to do without a place to live. Nor could I sleep well that night, as I relived the fire.

The next day, I went back to the burned-out house. Piles of damaged furnishings littered the lawn. Gaping windows revealed scorched interiors. I picked my way up the water-soaked back steps and walked through the broken rear door.

"Anybody here?" I shouted. No one answered, but I could hear voices, so I worked my way through several blackened rooms, still dripping with water, until I found several men in an area that was not so badly damaged.

"I'm a neighbor," I explained. "I came to see if I could help."

No one replied. I suspected they resented my intrusion.

"I really don't know what I can do," I added, "but I can help you out a little. There'll be more expenses than you know. Extra money will come in handy."

18

"I'll see you outside," one of the men answered slowly, leaving the others and leading me to the rear porch.

"Thanks. I don't know how it happened. Maybe the kid. He's five," he said as he took a rag out of his pocket and wiped his forehead. "My wife is not well, I had just left home, they told me when I got to work. I thought they were kidding . . . I just had a couple of shots to steady my nerves. My hands won't stop shaking . . ."

We talked for a while, and I gave him the money and left. But it was not really easy to leave, for the smell of smoke clung to my clothes and the sight of the gutted rooms remained in my mind.

But my concern had to be pushed aside, for it was getting late and I had an appointment at the local hospital where I was scheduled to be the day's volunteer chaplain. I arrived there at noon and put on a white jacket that allowed me around the floors without question. I was prepared to listen, to encourage, to pray, and to share my own faith as a source of help for others. I expected to call on about ten patients.

When I asked at a nurses' station for suggestions about who needed a visit, one of the nurses said, "The patient in Room 214 is pretty depressed. She's been told about an unsuspected tumor."

When I entered the room, I asked, "How are things going today?"

"Not too well," came the alert answer. "I am to be transferred to another hospital for more examinations. I am afraid I have some real trouble."

"Could you tell me more?" I queried.

"I've been having stomach pains. The doctors have given me a lot of tests, but they do not seem to know the whole story. Did you say you're a chaplain? I see you have a badge."

"Yes, I visit people when they come to the hospital."

"Do you have any place where we could talk alone?" she asked, looking uncomfortably at the patient in the bed next to her.

"We have a prayer room," I replied. "As a matter of fact, it's on this floor."

"Can anybody go there?"

"It's always open. Would you like to see it?"

With that, the woman reached for her robe, slid out of bed, and walked with me to the small room at the end of the corridor.

For a moment or two we just sat and looked around.

19

"What are the books and pamphlets in the rack?" she asked.

"They're prayers and stories about faith and God," I explained as I picked one out and read a couple of short prayers to her.

"One of those prayers referred to school teachers," she observed. "I'm a teacher, too."

So we talked for a few moments about her school and her family. Then I remembered that she had been the one to suggest the prayer room, so I asked what prayer meant to her.

"Prayer means a great deal," she replied. "I have found it one of the most profound influences in my life. It has helped me find strength to live through a number of difficult situations."

"Would you like to pray now?" I asked.

What followed was an experience I will long remember. The woman sat in silence for several moments and then spoke in a calm, poised, personal manner. She seemed in communication with a source upon which she relied for strength as well as direction. She gave thanks for her husband, prayed that her children might learn well in school, that her neighbors might watch over her home and family while she was in the hospital. She gave thanks for the nurses, for the skill of the doctors, for the men and women who made the hospital possible. She expressed appreciation for the care of friends and mentioned several of them by name. Finally, she prayed for herself, that she might help herself and be filled with the power to live a good life. She seemed to choose each word with sensitivity and yet the words came easily as if from experience.

When she had finished, she sat quietly for some time, apparently not wanting to interrupt the spirit or feeling. When she got up, I walked her back to her room and bed; then she just waved to me, as if to say, "Thanks a lot, I feel better now. You can go."

It was strange leaving her. Somehow I felt I had been in the presence of a special person. There was something about her and her faith that gave me a sense of peace in myself.

After a number of other calls, none of which were so personally rewarding, I left the hospital to return to my office. I did not suspect that my day was to be dramatically changed again.

As I passed the local police station, a woman came out sobbing uncontrollably. I was surprised to recognize her as one of the new people who had been attending my church recently. She was the wife of a man who was a suspected professional burglar. I

20

immediately thought something had happened concerning the husband and I was partly right.

"It's my husband," she explained after I had asked her if I could help. "He threw me out of the apartment. I can take his beating, but he's got my baby. He gets wild when he's drunk. He told me if I went to the police, he'd get even by taking her away. I went to the cops anyway and just now they told me to see my lawyer. Who has a lawyer? Not me. What am I goin' to do?"

I probed around for more information. Yes, she had a friend who would take her in for the night. Yes, the friend knew a lawyer. Yes, the husband might harm the child, but had not done so before, even though he got drunk a lot.

"You go to your friend," I told her," and I'll call you tomorrow." I felt that they had an ordinary marital quarrel and gambled on that, hoping that the husband was not really in a threatening mood and I was not allowing a tragedy to take place.

Fortunately, I was right, for when I phoned the following day, she explained, "Yeah, he brought the baby back; he couldn't take care of her and work too. I'm going back this afternoon. Thanks for your help. I hope I can get to church Sunday."

So that was my day. In the morning, I had visited despairing victims of a burned home; at noon, I had shared in a high experience of prayer; in the afternoon, I had befriended a threatened wife.

In the eyes of many people, I suppose I really did nothing.

"Anybody could do what you did," they might say. "It doesn't take much to just stand around and listen to people!"

Indeed. I had not been a trained fireman saving a home. I had not been an accredited physician advising a patient. Nor had I been a professional lawyer counseling a fearful wife. Such "doers" and "movers" are important!

But from the pastor's point of view, there is much more to these stories.

The fire may have been out in the house but the frightening memory of it may not leave the home owner's mind! Bad dreams, recurring flashes of fear of flames, and despondency over lost personal possessions continue. In fact, after the fire is over, the pastor's work just begins, as he or she may spend weeks or months helping the person through the processes of adjustment.

Doctors can walk into patient's rooms with bad news and walk out again, sometimes leaving the sick person more disturbed of mind than of body. Then the pastor's work begins: to help individuals face disappointment, severe curtailment of life's activities, or even death. The doctor may have the unpleasant task of telling a person that a serious operation is needed, but the pastor has the larger and longer work of enabling the patient to face the uncertain future with faith and hope.

Clergy know that crises are really opportunities! When life is disrupted, it may be just what is needed for change to take place. Shared suffering can be, with God's help, the beginning of an even deeper and more meaningful life. It is the pastor's work to see that apprehensive patients interpret crisis in this creative way.

Let not the pastor feel he or she is any less important than a firefighter, a lawyer, or even a doctor. Fires may sometimes prove the fallacy of putting too much trust in possessions. The loss of material things may open lives to more lasting values, like those which are the province of the pastor.

The lawyer may help to bring about justice, but justice is not necessarily the highest goal in life. It is the pastor's role to sow the seeds of belief in the ultimate victory of God, in order to help people survive the inevitable injustices of everyday living.

Nor is health the greatest gift of life. As important as health is, there are many persons who find that ill health opens emotional and spiritual doors to the mystical insights that come with suffering. Poor health can force us to find sustaining spiritual resources we never appreciated before.

So there may be three life gifts: possessions, justice, and health. But there is one other that is more valuable than all these three—the gift of faith and hope. A person can live successfully without things, without justice, and without health. But few of us can really exist without faith and hope. There is no more important task in life than calling faith and hope into being, and this is the role of the pastor!

Hallowed
Be Thy Name

So, whether you eat or drink,
or whatever you do,
do all to the glory of God. (1 Corinthians 10:31)

The Preacher

Those of us who answer the call to ministry are known by many different names: "pastor," "Rev.," "Reverend," "Doctor," and sometimes just "Joe" or "Sally." But the one that identifies all of us is "preacher."

Though most of our week is filled with responsibilities including calling on the sick, counseling people in trouble, attending committee meetings to keep the church active, representing God at various civic affairs, and fulfilling denominational programs to raise mission money, most of us spend anywhere from four to eight hours a week in the preparation of the Sunday sermon. A clergyperson who emphasizes preaching takes more hours than this.

Preaching every seven days is not easy. Though it is inspiring to testify to the "saving power of Christ," there are Sundays when we just don't feel like conducting any kind of worship.

I am reminded of the young man who told his wife one Sunday that he did not want to go to church. She replied, "You've go to go; you're thirty years old and you're the minister!"

Procrastination and laziness are not the only reasons why we tire of preaching. Answering the needs and demands of a congregation, struggling with our own faith, battling with members who see things differently, and suffering ennui from too many community commitments—all these exhaust a pastor's energy. But we know the congregation will be waiting. Some of them will need a word of faith, of forgiveness, or of direction. So we go.

For me, entering the pulpit has always been a moment of self-examination and judgment. The pulpit asks of me, "Are you worthy to stand in this place? Has your life during the past week been moral enough to give you the right to preach about the Christian life?" There have been occasions when I could not pass that test.

At such times, my public pastoral prayer probably revealed my inner battles, at least to those who knew me well. But still, the prayer helps me restore my spiritual strength, and by the end of the service a sense of being forgiven often takes hold of me. Sometimes, as I preach the Good News, I feel renewed to such an extent that I want to stop and thank the worshipers. Thus the weekly responsibility of conducting worship is a recurring discipline which lifts my life above what it might have been.

Perhaps the same can be said for church members. Most people need prompting to help keep faith alive. Sometimes reminders even turn into ways of life. A friend once put it this way:

I used to see my church attendance as a spiritual wake-up call. I needed the regular checkup of a Sunday morning. Church was a weekly reminder of God. Then I realized that faith and God were with me all week. It changed my life.

Another church member explained:

As a steel salesman, I meet all kinds of people. Although many of them are honest and hard-working, I can tell you that the world out there is a pretty messy place. I come to the church in order to be reminded about what the world is supposed to be like.

It is awesome to be a preacher. When I consider that I am expected to speak for God, I know I must be more than I am to be a resource to people on their journey toward the Kingdom. As such I have responsibility in the tradition of the prophets to proclaim "Thus saith the Lord!"

However, even as I do I must admit that I may be wrong! Being human, I am tainted by my imperfections and thus an uncertain medium for the will of God. The most I can say is, "I preach the Word as I understand it today. Prayer and God may reveal more to me tomorrow, but now I must state, 'This is the Way of the Lord.'"

Like all pastors, I preach what God directs me to say. I do so in the faith that the Lord will surely destroy the chaff when I err and save the seed when I speak the truth.

Those of us who believe in God are expected to be measuring rods of the present and prophets of the future. It is the greatest cause to which clergy and laypersons can be called!

The Sermon

Some of us write our sermons, memorize the material and then preach without referring to the manuscript. Others read what they may have composed the week before in the study. Some subscribe to the commercial sources which provide a new sermon, complete with illustrations to choose from, every week. Some of us become so busy with parish matters that we get to sermon preparation only on Saturday evening. However, most of us have found that such late planning produces too much anxiety and not enough depth. Unless we "own" a sermon as our own thought and prayer, it is usually not very influential. Of course, there are those who so believe in the inspiration of the Lord that they prepare a little and preach a lot, unfortunately overlooking the fact that much of what they say is repetitious.

Another plan, which I have sometimes followed, is to establish topics for Sundays of the coming year while I am studying during my summer vacation. Then, in the intervening months I develop the subjects by reading, collecting significant quotations and illustrations, and then meditating upon the scripture. But no matter how I prepare a sermon, I leave the manuscript behind when I enter the pulpit. If I cannot preach it from the heart, without notes, it is not real. I must be a living testimonial of what I say, if at all possible. I have also found it helpful to rehearse before the empty church early Sunday morning. It helps to flood my words with the Spirit so that preaching the word may be more authoritative.

Many of us use different styles of sermons even as our Lord called people through stories, discussions, confrontations, and informal talks. We use dialogue sermons, interview sermons, poetic sermons, sermons in song, or even read sermons preached by others in history.

As pastors, we can often tell how a sermon has been received, even if no one comments. If people stand around and talk after a service, it usually means they have heard something worth discussing and they want to check with friends. On the other hand, if they are quick to leave, they probably have been turned off, and their negative response has taken the edge off their interest in any further fellowship.

How to deliver a sermon presents problems, but a far greater concern is what to preach about! Often I find I must confront my congregation with what they do not want to hear; as a friend explained:

> I am paid to preach the gospel, and I preach it out of my own conscience. If the shoe fits and they feel uncomfortable, that's not my problem. If the judgment of the scripture makes them feel guilty, I can't help that. When I'm in the pulpit, I must preach the word as I understand it. Sometimes it is not I who am speaking, but I feel a strange presence within me, directing what I am saying.

Every preacher has stories to tell about the power of the spoken word. We have known members to walk out of church in the middle of a sermon, either because they objected to the message or felt under conviction by the word and thought they were being personally attacked. Sometimes, we are assaulted ourselves, after the sermon, because people think we are too political, not political enough, or have misrepresented the "true word."

And there are the light-hearted occasions, too. During a Christmas service an elderly layman in one of my churches stood up and asked to speak. He said he wanted to report some "angels." I did not know whether he had received a vision, or was wandering-of-mind and might embarrass himself, but I let him continue. It turned out that he had been visited at his home by the caroling church choir, whom he called "angels" and he just wanted to thank them.

There are serious sides to preaching a sermon. It would be a rare pastor who has not felt called to tell a congregation what they don't want to hear: that they are prejudiced, that they are too pocketbook protective, that they are cold in spirit, or that they are unfaithful and immoral. I don't know of any pastor who has not preached in such a confrontive way that the ire and reaction of the members has not been felt for weeks. Pastors can be crucified for the truth too! However, we are called of God and in that power we preach again and again.

But rising to that nobility every successive week is difficult and all of us admit that there are times when "another sermon" is a real downer. One conscientious pastor put it this way:

Sometimes I don't want to preach at all because I don't give a damn. Sometimes I preach because it's just plain ego-satisfying. Sometimes I'm preaching to myself, with the congregation listening in. Sometimes, when I'm in the pulpit, the heavens open, and like Moses of old, God supplies the words.

Whatever the situation, pastors are called to provide a lamp unto the feet of the parish. They have to be aware that where there is no vision the people will perish. It is an awesome task, that of preaching a sermon, a task supported by the grace of God but sometimes an experience which drains all of the faith we have. It is not easy to be God's Ambassador.

God's Ambassador

There are subtle stimulants
that every minister knows:
      organ fanfare, choir support,
      filled pews, pulpit status,
      and the sanctuary body-warmth from
          many worshipers.

If all these were the pathway to Heaven,
      we could storm God's gates with rituals,
      or bring in the Kingdom with numbers.

The congregation demands the role of "Pastor"
      to be both priest and prophet:
      scintillating and profound,
      actor and orator,
      penetrating and humorous,
      challenging and comforting,
      filled with the Spirit,
      yet human enough to understand.

So we rise in each service:
pouring out our heart and soul
digging publicly into the depths of our Spirit:
      in the faith that some power
      of the Eternal Word
      will come through to feed the throng.

We must not confuse numbers with Faith, or
      attention with commitment,
      congratulations with sincerity.
      "Enjoyed the sermon, pastor," could mean
      "Notice me here, today!"
      Many of the most faithful attenders
      may only say "Good Morning, Reverend."

The choir's special anthem
   no longer fills the sanctuary.
Families take their children
   and go home for Sunday dinner.
An usher or two remain
   to count money and talk about golf.
The sexton clicks the locks
   making an echoing sound in the empty halls.

The central figure,
      sits alone in an inner office
      marked "Pastor,"
      with tears.

A sign on the study wall proclaims:
   "O Jerusalem . . . how often would I have gathered
   your children together as a hen gathers her brood
   under her wings, and you would not!" (Matt. 23:37)

On Preaching the Word

Preaching is more than stating ideas and opinions. What we preachers say is a reflection of who we are. We leak out our feelings and there are those who can understand us more than we realize.

John Woolman, the American Quaker, sometimes attended Indian services of worship. He was asked why he went, especially since he could not understand the language.

"I go," he explained, "because I like to hear where the words come from."

It is more important for a pastor to have a faith-filled inner life than an exceptional skill as an orator.

The Dutch theologian and scholar, Erasmus (1466-1536), for example, packed his Geneva church because of his extraordinary theology and faith, not his delivery. He was so nearsighted that his face almost touched the page of his manuscript as he read his prepared text.

Good preaching is a matter of the Spirit and depends upon the condition of the soul.

An American psychotherapist was visiting friends in Mexico. One Sunday, he was invited to attend their church. He found the Mexican music and the order of worship different, but he had to ask what the pastor was preaching about because he did not understand Spanish.

"It was a sermon on love," his friends replied.

"He may have been talking about love," explained the therapist, "but his body postures, the inflections in his voice, his facial expressions, and his gestures lead me to conclude that, in reality, he is a very angry man."

A pastor's personal life is the foundation upon which his preaching must be built. No pastor can live one way and preach another for long. As difficult as it is, we are called to live the faith as well as to preach it.

Rev. Mr. Brown was a conscientious minister. He had proven effective and faithful for many years, but as time passed the congregation noticed a change in his preaching and in his personality. He seemed increasingly distant, until one day he opened his heart to some close friends.

"I hate to admit it," he confessed, "but I've been a gambler all my life, more recently a compulsive gambler. I've even been able to keep it hidden but in the last few years my debts have gotten the better of me, and I'm in trouble. I must ask for your compassion, if you'll give it. I know my personal problem has been affecting my preaching. I can hide no longer. Will you help me?"

Brown's friends took the matter to the church's board. They pointed out that he had been a fine pastor for many years and that perhaps it was a chance for the church to help him as he had helped so many of them. The board gave him a leave of absence, they promised support for his family, and then hired an interim pastor to fill the pulpit.

A number of months passed and then quietly Brown returned. But he was not the same. The painful therapy sessions and the hours of personal prayer and meditation had created a new man. In fact, his sermons revealed his experience of "death" and to the joy of his congregation they sensed a whole new spirit of faith. They became aware, too, of their roles as persons who were willing to forgive. The example of Brown's fall from grace and renewal of faith was not lost on many of the members who, in times of gossip, admitted, "If he can be changed, perhaps the Lord can help me too!"

But Brown's story serves another purpose. It reminds us that what affects our inner souls also influences our outer lives. If we do not have the Spirit, either as preachers or as church members, the world will find out soon enough! On the other hand, if we are grounded faithfully in the love of God, the bread we cast upon the waters will come back to us a hundredfold. But it must be good "bread."

"The Baker"

I know a man who has been a baker for a number of years.

Of course, the flour that he uses really comes from nature, from Creation. His role as baker is to mix, flavor, knead and bake, then to get people to buy.

One day I asked him about the bread.

"Is it as good as you say it is?" I asked. "Give me an honest answer."

"Well, I'll tell you," he replied. "It is good bread, there's no doubt about that. But some days I make a pretty bad batch and people don't like it."

"I don't follow what you are saying. Tell me more," I urged.

"What I mean is this," he continued. "The taste of bread is dependent upon the way it is made. Some days, I'm just not myself. Perhaps I have been distracted, thinking of other things, or maybe even feeling guilty about something I've done. You could say I lost touch with myself. Then my bread is not the best."

31

"I really didn't expect you to make a private confession," I interrupted, fearing that he might both embarrass himself as well as me.

"You don't understand," he added. "I believe there's a relationship between how a man lives and what he accomplishes, between his morality and his ability to make good bread, to use a personal illustration. There's a connection between how I conduct my personal life and my ability as a baker. When my life is not right, when I feel bad about myself, when I may feel guilty, I'm not inclined to do things well. I may forget something. I might not bake the batch just right."

"On the other hand, when I'm 'up' with a good feeling about who I am, because something good has happened or I have won a battle with temptation, I'm more in control of things. I'm clear-headed about carrying out every detail. The mix is good, the texture is OK, and my bread turns out as it should."

I thanked my friend for his frankness and left, relfecting on what he had said. Then I realized that all pastors are bakers.

We are "bakers of the word," the bread of life. We take the basic ingredient, the word, which has come to us from the Creator. We mix and flavor it, and then offer the word, as the bread of life, to nourish individuals and congregations.

If the pastor (the baker) is tainted with "sin," the resultant anxiety may affect the preparation and thus sour the "bread." A congregation may be able to taste the sourness of a sermon prepared under the influence of guilt.

On the other hand, if a pastor prepares the word with clean hands and a pure heart, he or she may produce bread which will be truly nourishing.

I suspect that some church members can tell the way the "baker" has lived during the week, by the taste of the "bread" they receive on Sunday.

Pastors need to be clear channels of grace and need to be clean vessels in order to carry the word to God's children, but the Word does not depend upon us alone. Sometimes God uses broken or imperfect vessels: Moses was imperfect, King David was imperfect, and Paul called himself "the chief of sinners." Still they interpreted the message of God.

We need to be as good "bakers" as we can, always relying on God to use us.

32

The Office of Pastor

I used to be the minister of the biggest and wealthiest church in a well-to-do suburb. I represented power and social prestige. I was important because many of the movers and shakers of the town were my parishioners. I was cultivated by community people who were impressed with the influence of my congregation. I was asked to serve on civic committees. I officiated at society weddings. I was invited to family anniversaries. I was called upon to bless secular meetings.

All of that was possible, of course, because I held the office of pastor, a professional standing I had earned long before. Indeed, the process had been a long one. I had been interviewed for the position. I had agreed to the job description. I had been recommended by the search committee and then voted on by the whole congregation. Then I was installed in a special ceremony and recognized by the denomination of which the local church was a part. Thus I was invested in the office and thereafter addressed as "Reverend."

I entered upon my work with that congregation expecting many challenges. I was not disappointed. I soon found myself at odds with a few powerful members over the issue of race because I supported the policy of more civil rights for minorities, who, I thought, were being denied their God-given privileges of equality.

"I don't agree with you at all," an irate board chairman informed me one evening. "And just to show you how much I feel about this, if you keep on preaching this way, I may leave the church."

But he didn't. Later he told me that although he did not support what I said, nevertheless he respected the church, and he respected me for preaching my Christian convictions.

During another period of that pastorate, I spoke frequently about peace. I was for more peace initiatives and less military sword-rattling. I felt I was faithfully witnessing to the teachings of Jesus on the issue, but a number of folks told me they interpreted Jesus and peace in a different way. However, they said, they looked to the church and pastor to present the scriptures with learned authority, and they would tolerate my viewpoint because I was "The Minister."

On another occasion I was visiting an elderly neighbor lady whose church had a new pastor.

"What do you think of him?" I asked.

"He's a fine young man," she replied. "He'll learn. They come an' go. I've seen lots filling our pulpit in my time. Some are good an' some aren't, but they're all called to preach the word of the Lord an' that makes 'em more than they are."

Indeed, the authority of the office endows pastors with more influence and power in the eyes of the public than they may suspect. Their words become weighted with the status of the position they hold. The office can make the preacher.

I became aware of just how true this is when I left a church in the town where I had been "The Pastor" and moved to another situation twenty miles away. I served the new church for a number of years. Then, by chance, I moved back to the former community where I had been so well known. This time, however, I was not "The Pastor" but just another community resident.

The difference between having a title and not having one, in the same town and among the same people, was dramatic!

Although a few former friends remained personally close, most of my previous community acquaintances dropped away. Perhaps we would have grown apart anyway over the intervening years, but the fact was that I was no longer a community figure. I no longer represented power or position or status. The man in the street, who had formerly cultivated my friendship, now had no need of me.

The difference between being a community figure, as most clergy become, and being a plain resident like everyone else, points up the significance of the minister's office. It was not me they had invited in those previous years, it was my position. It was not my faith which had brought recognition to my name, but my title. The distinction raises a significant concern for all ministers or pastors:

How many clergy understand the difference between who they are, and what the title of their office may lead them to think they are?

I suggested earlier that "the office can *make* the preacher!" That is true but the reverse is true also, "The office can *break* the preacher."

Rev. John Smith is a conscientious, faith-filled minister. He speaks well and is admired by his congregation. He is ambitious to be a good pastor and to move up in the ranks of the church. Everyone seems to be impressed with John, except his wife.

"He's never home," she complains. "All he thinks about is the church and his success in it. I don't even know him as a person any more, and to tell the truth, I don't think the church people know him either. The time that he should spend with me and the kids, he's over at the church planning meetings or doing committee work."

Another evaluation of John comes from his best friend.

"John knows he is a well-liked pastor who is on his way to a successful career, but that's not enough in my book. There's not enough depth or personality to John. He ought to cultivate himself or his marriage more. I hope he gets away from the office and finds John some day. If he's going to be a good pastor in any church, he must know himself first."

Every minister needs to discover the difference between office and self.

. . . .

If there is conflict between office and self, there is also tension between career and family. As we have mentioned, many pastors give more of their lives to the former than to the latter as is tragically expressed in a letter many a pastor could write; unfortunately too late to do any good to himself but which could possibly be helpful counsel to new pastors.

A Letter to a Friend

Dear Mike,

You asked in your last letter how things go with me in the ministry. Let me tell you honestly.

Like all ministers, I have been challenged to be more faithful, to serve the church without counting the cost, as did our Lord, to support my peers, and to be committed in spirit.

I have attended conferences, special programs, and emergency meetings. I have taken part in campaigns, filled positions on boards, worked on projects for the denomination, and often put in more than sixty hours a week for my parish.

I have married hundreds of couples, counseled more than that. I have taught classes, chaired committees, attended study sessions, and written dozens of official minutes.

I have been encouraged by my superiors to be action-minded, spiritually centered, organized in calling, effective in administration, and successful at money-raising.

Now many years after beginning my ministry, I discover that I know many sides of the church, but, alas, very few sides of my own family. I have known conference rooms, but I barely know my own living room. I have met hundreds of fine people but still have to really meet my own wife and children.

Some church members point to the crucifixion of Christ and speak about his sacrifice. I tell you, it is not limited to the martyrs who were burned at the stake in foreign lands by cruel pagans. It can happen, and does, to present-day pastors in all kinds of churches.

Scripture says, "Her children shall rise up and call her blessed" (Prov. 31:28) Not mine. They rise up to reject the church. They know so little about me, they no longer know how to ask. Rise up to bless me? Are you kidding? They have risen up to leave this minister's household as soon as they could.

Mike, you ask about my ministry. The ministry is fine, but I have lost a family in pursuit of meeting the expectations of ministry. . . . Maybe this letter will help another pastor to do it all in a better way.

Sincerely yours,

On the Sacraments

While all churches may invite and encourage the laity to preach, the sacraments of baptism and the Lord's Supper are usually the province of the professional minister.

Sacraments are rites specifically ordered by Christ.

"And Jesus came and said to them . . . 'make disciples of all nations, baptizing them . . .'" (Matt. 28:18-19).

"The Lord Jesus . . . took bread . . . and said 'This is my body which is for you. Do this in remembrance of me.'" (1 Cor. 11:23-24)

Baptism

Baptism is the initiatory rite of membership in the church and acceptance into the family of God, by which one begins the journey toward newness of life and resurrection. The efficacy of the sacrament is not affected by the moral character of the pastor who baptizes but rather by the grace of God's action. I gave thanks for this theological point very soon after I was ordained into the ministry.

I was asked by an actor and his actress wife if I would baptize their child. I told them I would be glad to do so, even though it was going to be my very first baptism. I was nervous about the sacrament and scrupulously kept reading the service from the minister's manual. But that anxiety of inexperience was not my only problem. Every time I looked at the actress, I lost my cool. She was the most beautiful woman I had ever seen. I would look at her, so lovingly attentive to her infant, and I would lose my place in my book.

When the service was over, the father thanked me for the baptism and then added, with a wry smile:

"The baby was a boy, not a girl, as you kept saying in your service."

I hope that beautiful actress, who has undoubtedly increased the heart beats of a multitude of admirers, knows her theology well enough to remember that baptism depends upon the grace of God's initiative, rather than the spiritual experience (or in my case, inexperience) of the officiating minister.

Even though I was embarrassed and have had many a smile about that baptism, I know that I was, even if inadequately, carrying on one of the foundations of the Christian church, that we should all be baptized in Jesus' name (Matt. 28:18-19).

It is good to know, too, that pastors do have insurance against the novice conduct of worship, as the employment of liturgy of the church helps to overcome our shallowness. More and more it is becoming customary for the witnessing congregation to repeat the great creeds of the church with the ceremony, thus identifying themselves with the meaning of the sacrament and also recommitting themselves to what the special family may be experiencing.

Of course baptism is more than being sprinkled or even immersed in water, with the theological overtone that in being buried in water and then rising again we are cleansed from our inherited sins and we start on the journey to eternal life. The water that we use is an outward sign of an inward grace.

Baptism is also of the Spirit, as the forerunner of our Lord, John, pointed out: "I baptize you with water . . . he will baptize you with the Spirit" (Matt. 3:11).

This baptism has affected my life. I experience this cleansing again and again as I find the Spirit touching my life with new meaning and a renewed sense of God's presence. This baptism is an ongoing experience. The Spirit is continually baptising my life, revealing me to myself in unexpected ways, and renewing my sensitivity to the call of God in ever more meaningful prayers. This process of being mentally, soulfully, and spiritually cleansed again and again refreshes my faith and draws me, with ever more humility, into the presence and security of God.

As a creation and thus a child of God, and as a follower of Jesus Christ, I was once baptized with water unto repentance and ever since baptized again and again, in search of that repentance, by the Holy Spirit.

. . . .

Protestants recognize one other sacrament, in addition to Baptism—Holy Communion, the central celebration of the Christian church!

Holy Communion

"It's going to be an easy Sunday this week," the young minister observed, "It's communion; no sermon to prepare, just bread and wine to pass around."

I was shocked at the nonchalant attitude toward the sacrament, but I could not help wondering if this is the way many church members think; just an unusual memorial ceremony with pieces of bread (or yeast-free wafers) and tiny glasses of wine (or grape juice) which are too small to be used for shot glasses and not big enough to really catch the bouquet of the spirits, but which are used as symbols for a memorial for Jesus, the Christ.

I must admit, however, that appreciation of the sacrament has come slowly to me. Celebrating the memory of our Lord seemed logical at first but did not explain why others feel Communion is so significant. Then I began to sense the sacrament calling me to a new awareness of community, in fact a Holy Community, where people love each other even as Christ loves us. Later, I experienced a deeper commitment to our Lord as I took the bread and wine in the sight of the whole congregation and realized I was making a public statement about my loyalty to Christ.

With each Communion, my understanding has deepened, until now I sense that the bread and wine (the body and blood) are actually spiritual nourishments for my soul and spirit.

Sometimes, when I am the celebrant, I feel like Peter in that I understand the event and have the keys to the Kingdom plus the authority to call worshippers to this sublime community of faith. At other times, I am almost unable to conduct the service because of a feeling of awe and unworthiness in the presence of Christ.

Sometimes, I despair because Communion is in such contrast to where people really are today. So many worshippers seem lonely. They come to church thinking that the service will create a supporting fellowship for them. And it should, but our traditional orders of worship and liturgies do not bring about real meeting, and people go away more isolated than they came.

As a pastor, I feel Holy Communion should be a living experience with others. Unfortunately, so many of our celebrations of the sacrament seem to be confining and directed toward the past.

Some of our services are in architecturally old sanctuaries, so often closed in by stained glass windows which shut out, instead of reaching out to, the world. Our traditional liturgies, often in archaic language, seem to reflect ancient history instead of pointing us to new fields of faith. Our formal Orders of Worship seem to restrict people's emotions instead of releasing them.

Holy Communion is the call to believers in Christ to transcend the world, to live a new life in him, an existence of faithful creative relationships. How mystical the celebration is! How it defies adequate explanation!

It has been the difficulties of interpretation, especially to young people, that has moved me to offer the sacrament in ways which I feel may be more relevant to their lives and to the times. I have used stamps instead of bread, and quarters instead of wine, in an effort to help youth understand age-old symbols. I have broken Communion out of old established molds by offering it in new forms. I have felt the meaning of the sacrament called for it to be moved from institutionalism to a freer and more creative personal experience.

"Stamps, Quarters, and a Card Table"

I was once asked, as ministers are, to celebrate Communion with a group of high schoolers. I wanted to make the experience more relevant to them, so I looked for a symbol that would help them see the sublime willingness of Christ to give himself to save others.

I thought of my hobby of collecting American postage stamps. I used to study how they were designed, printed, watermarked, used, and cancelled. I was a stamp researcher. Over the years, I have collected a few sheets of various commemorative issues.

What if I used some of those stamps instead of bread and wine? After all, when our Lord shared the bread he was using it as a symbol of giving of himself, the sacrifice of love, for the benefit of others. Could I not say the same thing with my stamps?

So when the service came to the time for Communion, I made this proposal to the students.

"Here is a special sheet of historical stamps. I have kept them for years. I could continue to save them for myself, but I feel that would be selfish. So I'm going to break up the sheet and give a few stamps to each one of you. In this way, I'll share my hobby, and thus part of myself, with you."

Their response was enthusiastic.

"Thanks, I'd like to have a part of a stamp collection. I'd save it too," said one student.

I cautioned, "Don't hoard my gift as a souvenir. Put the stamps to use. Though old, they are still good for postage. So mail a letter to a friend to whom you have not written for a long time. Use my gift as a way of sharing part of yourself with someone else!"

At first, everyone seemed pleased with having the unusual stamps. They looked at them carefully and handled them with interest. They quickly thanked me for my generosity, but soon they had other reactions.

"I can't take your stamps," one girl explained. "You have saved them for your collection!"

"Your example means a lot to me," another added. "I'm going to keep my stamp to remind me of this occasion."

A third youth protested, "I really don't understand why you want to give your stamps away."

I tried to explain the comparison between the offering of a special possession and the offering by Christ, but the sacrifice of one's self for the benefit of another person is foreign to our materialistic society and therefore difficult to comprehend.

We need additional illustrations to help youth understand the depth of commitment the Christian has to others, even as Christ gave himself for us.

. . . .

On another occasion when a group wanted Holy Communion, I used money as the symbol of sharing.

"See all the money I have," I boasted as I stood before a youth group and poured a handful of quarters from one hand to the other.

"I like my money. It makes me feel rich. I could keep it all, but I am not going to. Believe it or not, I'm going to share with you. I'm going to give each of you a part of my wealth in quarters. Here, take a couple, and spend them on someone you like. You're not to keep any for yourselves. You must find someone to give to. And when you do, tell them you care for them."

As before, the reaction was dramatic.

"I cannot take your money," said one, "You earned it, not me! What have I done to deserve your money?"

Another suggested, "You make me feel guilty. Here, take your quarters back."

A third high schooler was even more critical: "Too bad," he cried. "You gave us only quarters. If you had given us dollars, I'd have been more convinced!"

. . . .

Communion, of course, is more than experiencing the giving of ourselves for the sake of someone else, even as Christ gave himself that we might understand the reality of love, and the depths to which love will go to save.

Communion is "community"—the meeting between persons, the intermingling of hopes and fears, joys and sorrows, despair and hope. Martin Buber suggested, "All real living is meeting."

So, besides formal services, I have offered Communion in still another way. On a Lenten evening service with the sacraments, I arrange for a small table to be placed in the center aisle. On it is a solitary large candle, and next to it are only two chairs. Then, after the elements have been blessed at the altar or Communion table, I tell the parishioners that soon the lights in the sanctuary will be almost extinguished, at which time they are invited to come, two by two, to the small table, where I will put the bread and wine. They are to seat themselves opposite each other, and, in the silence, serve each other! I invite couples to share Communion in this way, friends to serve friends as well as strangers.

If all real living is meeting, this type of Communion certainly emphasizes the caring intimacy to which Jesus calls us. Couples report that for the first time in all their married lives, they have given each other the Blessed Sacrament. Friends find a deeper relationship of their church membership. The witnessing congregation sees Holy Communion as more than something received, it is an intimate giving and receiving between two living souls who are being bound together for the moment (and longer) in the name of Christ.

The Importance of Calling

Questionnaires often ask congregations, "What is the most important part of your minister's work?" Almost always church members will reply, "Calling."

One of the most frequent criticisms of young pastors is that they do not call enough. A cleric may be a poor preacher, but if he or she is conscientious in making home and hospital calls, the congregation may overlook weakness in the pulpit.

Yet many clergy dislike to call. We are lazy. We forget that one of the best ways to make sermons significant is to listen personally to the needs and interests of the congregation.

Making an effective call requires skill. Once when I was visiting in a hospital as part of a chaplain's program to see patients just before their operations, I introduced myself to an older man. He quickly replied, "Thanks for coming, but I'm not religious and I'm not interested in talking."

Such rejections occur from time to time. An experienced caller may recognize that the patient really wants to talk but is too emotionally upset. Chaplains know that sharing insecurity and talking about worries is one of the best ways to prepare for an operation, so I accepted his rejection and then, after a pause, added:

"I suspect things are pretty tough right now."

That began to unlock his pent-up fears. A half-hour conversation followed, during which we shared what it is to be afraid. I told him I, too, was afraid on occasion. We talked about his family and friends. I did not think prayer was called for, but when I left, the man thanked me for staying and said he hoped I would come back again.

Visiting patients needs to be done with care. Some hospitals have learned that it is dangerous to allow the preacher to call who begins with the note of judgment, "Are you ready to meet God?" or "Your sickness may be due to some sin in your life. Confession could cure you!" Most hospitals agree that such aggressive evangelism raises additional fears in minds already burdened with apprehension, and they do not allow such pastors to visit patients other than members of their own congregations.

On the other hand, calling on men in prison may require just such a confrontation. Visiting may be brief, despair may be great, time for reflection may be ample, and the number of visitors may be limited. So the impact of a caring pastor who comes directly to the point about a Christ who saves may be doubly significant. Indeed, the apostle Paul did some of his most effective work on prisoners as well as jailers by bluntly confronting them with the gospel. (See Acts 16:25-34.)

Visiting is not all seriousness. I recall the time I approached the Smith home on a pleasant summer afternoon. I had just rung the doorbell when I noticed a tiny window in the door, not unlike those in old-time speakeasies. I leaned forward to examine it more closely, when the inside curtains opened. There were Mrs. Smith and I, face to face, nose to nose, within inches of each other. The only trouble was that Mrs. Smith's face was covered with a rose-colored mud cream. She looked a sight, and her surprised expression at seeing me so near made matters worse. The curtains abruptly closed, but the door was not opened. Nor did I care to wait to see if it would. In some embarrassment, I fled down the front stairs. As I walked away I thought of how I could share the unexpected confrontation with Mrs. Smith when she next attended church. However, it was months before she came again. She did not mention the incident, and I, out of a sense of discretion, thought I should not either. Maybe some day we will both be able to laugh together about it.

On another occasion, I visited the Shermans' home even though I never liked to because they had such a bunch of wild kids. Everything went well until I got ready to leave.

"I think I had a hat when I came in," I told Mrs. Sherman.

"I do believe you did," she replied. "I'll see what happened to it."

Soon she came back with the hat in her hand, but she was wiping it off with a kitchen towel.

"I'm very embarrassed," she replied. "The children had it in the bathroom; they were filling it up with water from the toilet and then giving our dog a drink. I think your hat will be OK when it dries off."

When I left that home, I thought of the incident in *A Sentimental Journey,* written by Laurence Sterne in 1768, in which the local pastor falls backward into a pig sty. "Times don't change much," I thought.

Keeping Records of Calls and Events

The clergy are notoriously lax about record keeping, which is unfortunate because it pays such large dividends in human appreciation. For example:

It was nice to have the young couple come to the morning service, after so many years, and to bring the baby too.

"You remember us, Pastor?" they exuberantly exclaimed, proudly showing their child but not giving their names. I did remember the couple but not their name. I had been intimately involved in a family fight concerning their marriage. To not remember their names was very embarrassing.

"Excuse me," I interrupted. "I have a phone call to make. I will be right back."

But the subterfuge was of no use. I couldn't find their names anywhere in the office.

"Why don't I keep a log of official events?" I chided myself. "People need to be known."

Record keeping is such a simple thing. A pastor friend of mine always sends special greeting cards. He does this for hundreds of his one-time parishioners by dating his mail far in advance and having his secretary send the greetings on the proper date. No matter. I am encouraged by hearing from him. He remembers me and gives meaning to my life. I continue to remember him though I have forgotten so many others.

But that is not all I have forgotten! Sometime last year I helped Mrs. Smith through the loss of her husband to whom she had been married for forty years. It was a period of deep sharing and understanding, but I cannot remember the date. I did not put it down. Now I'm afraid that one of these days, Mrs. Smith will be saying:

"Just a year ago my husband died. I thought the pastor, of all people, would call. It would mean so much, but I guess he's too busy to remember!"

It is important for clergy to keep notes concerning particular calling situations. Of course they should be destroyed when a pastor leaves one congregation for another, in order to protect the privacy of counseling. But some incidents can be saved for their learning value as long as names are changed, as I have done in the following story.

"Stanley"

"Pastor could you come over? I need help with Stanley."

"Sure," I replied, recalling that Stanley, a young man of the congregation, had been in and out of mental hospitals many times. "What is the problem?"

"He's in the basement," my phone caller continued. "He's behind the furnace, and he won't come out. I think he has one of the kitchen knives."

On the way over to the home, I thought about Stanley. He had been in World War I and had been involved in a notoriously disastrous assault. In the middle of an all-out attack, he had turned and run for the rear. The military disgrace as well as a dishonorable discharge and the resultant loss of self-esteem had left him with a history of mental instability. This in turn caused his parents much pain and grief.

His father met me at the door.

"You'll have to be careful," he advised. "Stanley's got a long knife. I've tried to get him to put it down and come upstairs, but he won't listen to me. I thought maybe you could do something with him. He likes you, you know."

I laid my overcoat on the kitchen table, opened the cellar door and started down. It was quite dark.

"There are times," I thought, "when the ministry is more than sermons."

46

Although I could not see Stanley, I heard scuffling on the cement floor. It seemed to come from behind the furnace, as his father had thought. I had no way of knowing whether he still had the knife or what he planned to do with it.

"Stanley," I called softly. "This is Reverend Tom, your friend. I have come to see you."

There was no response.

"You can trust me, Stanley," I continued. "Remember, we have been friends for a long time."

No response.

I could think of no words to communicate with a man who obviously was in his own private world. But I knew I had to win his attention. I began to recite the Lord's Prayer. I thought it might give him the time he might need to adjust to my presence. Then I heard a scuffling noise and slowly Stanley appeared. He had the knife in his hand. He did not seem threatening, though I knew I could be fooled.

"I have come to be with you, Stanley," I said in a slow voice.

Perhaps it was the tone of my speech, the prayer, the time that he needed to get control of what he wanted to do; he began walking toward me slowly.

I let him narrow the distance between us, and then very carefully I reached out and took his empty hand. At the same moment, I reached for the knife. He gave it to me without protest.

"Let's go upstairs together," I suggested.

After several moments of uncertainty he climbed the stairs with me. Soon he was slouched in one of the kitchen chairs, and staring off into space, oblivious to either his father or me.

I talked with the father for some time. Could he meet Stanley's needs? If not, was he willing for me to help find an institution which would?

Later, Stanley was admitted to a hospital. He was their problem now, and I confess to being relieved. But I was thankful that my training for ministry had alerted me as to when (or when not) to seek additional professional resources. Sometimes pastors do not refer at all, to the detriment of parishioners in need.

Official Record Keeping

One of the chief responsibilities of every pastor is to call on those who need to be fed by the love of Christ, but again, many clergy are reluctant to visit parishioners as often as they should. Congregations should make sure that their pastors fulfill this aspect of ministry by expecting that they give an adequate account of calls on a regular reporting basis.

I keep a monthly record of my calls and regularly supply my church officers with my number of visits. If they ask for more information, I am glad to reply, but only up to a point. I do not reveal whom I have called on or for what reason. Pastoral calls need to be confidential.

But I keep a record for my own reasons as well. I find that a review of the total, by week or even by month, reveals to me how faithfully I am working. A poor month must be overcome. A period low in calls says something about my dedication. Am I becoming lazy? Am I working as hard for my people as I should?

Keeping the official church records is a duty no pastor should avoid. How many of us have answered the office phone only to hear:

"Pastor, this is Mrs. Doe. You do not know me because I was a member of your church years ago. Now I need to have a record of my baptism (wedding, etc.). Could you please send it to me right away?"

Finally, I wish someone had advised me, at the very beginning of my ministry, to keep a complete *Record Book of Weddings, Marriages, Deaths, and Memorable Dates.* Such events are the unforgotten milestones of every life. To overlook them in the lives of friends and parishioners detracts from a pastor's faithfulness. Everyone likes to be remembered on his or her birthday. Widows or widowers need to know that they are not forgotten by their church on dates of their personal sorrows. My influence as a counselor-pastor to young and old could be much more significant if I could remember people on those special days which they never forget.

Thy Kingdom Come

"Earth breaks up, time drops away
In flows heaven, with its new day."

—Robert Browning, "Christmas Eve," Sec. 10

Bringing in the Kingdom

There is probably no phrase in the Lord's Prayer which is as controversial as "Thy kingdom come, thy will be done" (Matt. 6:10).

Clergy and laypersons do not argue over the objective of the prayer. All of us want to see the Kingdom come and all of us want to know that God's will be done.

The controversy arises over "how" and "what"; *how* is the Kingdom to come and *what* is the will of God.

The answer is simple for those who say "Just read the Bible!" Indeed, pastors are confronted by parishioners who believe that the will of God is easy to understand because, "It says so right here in scripture in plain English!"

It takes patience to explain that Bible "plain English" has been derived from "Old English" of Shakespearean times. The King James Version (1611) was translated from inferior medieval manuscripts in Greek or Hebrew, with meanings often changing along the way.

Further explanation is necessary to point out that the Bible is history, poetry, prophecy, allegory, and fact; and that each must be read with appreciation for the various backgrounds which makes the literature complicated instead of plain.

Furthermore, "plain English" does not turn out to be so simple when faithful, devoted Christians read the exact scripture but come up with entirely different understandings of what it means.

Roman Catholics build the authority of the church and the pope on the Bible. Lutherans reject such authority in favor of personal justification by faith. Jehovah's Witnesses read the same book and say that God has dated the end of the world and the coming of the Kingdom, while others believe the Kingdom will not come until every individual is filled with the love of Christ.

The divisions run still deeper! Some pastors will not strive for peace because they are convinced that if things get bad enough, God will intervene, separate the sheep from the goats, and establish his Kingdom. Other clergy who read Bible tell us, "If you want peace, work for justice!"

There are deep differences over the role of women in the church, whether they should be ordained as pastors and priests. There are serious arguments concerning military preparedness and the extent to which it conforms to the will of God.

In summary, clergy are involved in all sorts of spiritual decisions when it comes to deciding the right way to bring in the Kingdom.

There are, however, some matters which appear to be at least of common concern to all clergy. One is the matter of prejudice. Every pastor meets prejudice: longtime church members who resent the proposals of newcomers, men who are prejudiced against the new role of women, youth whose inexperience prejudices them against the wisdom of senior citizens, and white persons who feel threatened if minorities even attend church for worship.

Each of us has had a battle with prejudice. A memorable one for me was with a respected church member who had all sorts of names for people he did not like: "coon," "spik," "dago," and a lot more. His attitude was a thorn in my flesh as his pastor.

"I Hate Minorities"

"I hate minorities," stung my ears.
"I'll get a baseball bat if they come into my block!"

I thought, "This man and I will never be friends."
Yet I knew I must live with him,
because he was a member of my congregation,
with whom I was called to make a blessed community.

So I forced myself to become acquainted,
and found the man had never known his father,
who was killed in war, and he had spent most of his life
caring for a crippled mother.

Reflection reminded me that I could pass the racial test,
but probably could not pass some others, as he had done.

I forgave him, and adjusted to his "fault,"
and hoped he would forgive me too.
So we became friends.

I continue to see those holes in his coat.
Possibly he notes the holes in mine.
We are both ill-clad pilgrims
On our way to the small wicket gate.

Confronting Prejudice

The answer to racial prejudice cannot always be forgiveness or accommodation, such as I found with my parishioner. A pastor must stand up to the sin of prejudice which continues to make the worship hour on Sunday morning the most segregated hour in the week. Every pastor must search his own conscience to determine just what stand he will take.

I had the privilege of being the pastor of a large suburban congregation. I felt the gospel expected me to preach about the opportunity for others in God's family and I did so. However, I discovered a ground swell of opposition as several members advised me to take a softer approach. A few gathered, without my knowledge, to plan for my removal. It was only because other friends in the parish stood firm for racial understanding that the revolt was stunted and I held my job.

As I look back upon those tense days, one part of the story needs to be added. During the whole battle within the congregation over race, I made it a point to respect adversaries as they respected me. I invited them to lead worship. I encouraged them to serve on church boards. I am convinced that it was the mutual respect we maintained for each other that allowed us to differ and yet continue to work together for the church.

But that does not suggest backing away from the serious American issue of prejudice. It is so thoroughly a part of our America that many who consider themselves good Christians are caught in the prejudice of our national life without realizing it.

The pastor faces two traditional methods of attacking prejudice. One way is to call people to an ever closer devotion to God, to encourage them to develop their spiritual life, to lead them in prayer, and to call them to care for the stranger because it is God's will. When people feel the love of God, they find courage to love others, even those against whom they are prejudiced.

Another method is the appeal to conscience and social responsibility. Make the congregation aware of the differences between those who have and those who have not, these inequalities being one of the sources of prejudice. Appeal to reason and to fairness and to people's sense of morality. Supply those who are prejudiced with the facts.

Both methods can lead all of us who are pastors into a deeper confrontation with one of the greatest sins of American life— racial prejudice.

There are those who feel that the topic of race prejudice is out of date, but such is not the case. Racial conflict has been a common problem throughout history. It will not disappear in our time. In fact, it may soon become a most serious issue because two-thirds of the people of the world are nonwhite. These races are making increasing demands upon those who are of the white ruling minority.

Anthropologists tell us that prejudice between races is a learned and cultivated attitude. It is not inherited. If this is true, it is the responsibility of all who believe in "one Lord, one faith, one baptism"(Eph. 4:5) to confront prejudice wherever we find it.

"Ghetto and Suburb"

(A suburbanite talks with a resident of the ghetto.)

Suburb: I don't like the inner city. Too many people on the streets.
Ghetto: Suburban living must be lonely. No one on the streets.

Ghetto: It's gotten so I don't understand half of the languages spoken around here.
Suburb: I sure hope we can keep the Spanish out of this town.

Suburb: We had a rubbish fire in the garage today. Even the house seemed to smell of smoke. We have rented rooms in a motel until the insurance company gets everything fixed up.
Ghetto: The flat below us burned out this afternoon. It sure smells awful in here, but I suppose we'll get used to it.

Suburb: Bye honey. I'll read the paper on the train on the way to the office. I love ya.
Ghetto: Bye honey. I'll be hanging 'round Ted's Place today. See ya. I love ya.

Ghetto: The smell from the alley is awful. It's been that way for weeks.
Suburb: Which day do they pick up the extra trash? I'll call Jack. He's on the village board. He'll see that the truck comes by.

Suburb: I don't see why the kids watch TV so much.
Ghetto: I know why the kids watch TV so much.

Suburb: Take the car to the bank drive-in and get this check cashed. We need some extra change.
Ghetto: Walk to the food store. See if we have enough to feed the family this week.

. . . .

Distinctions
Ghetto: Country-of-origin distinction.
Suburb: Social distinctions.

Corner Lots
Suburb: Filling stations
Ghetto: Taverns

Houses
Suburb: 10 beautiful rooms for 4 people
Ghetto: 10 beautiful people for 4 rooms

Justice
Suburb: "It serves me."
Ghetto: "It serves them."

Entertainment
Suburb: Eat out, health spa, basement bar. "I do what I want to do."
Ghetto: Eat in, the park, the tavern. "I do what I can do."

The Police
Ghetto: Power of the Establishment to keep us in line.
Suburb: Power of the Establishment to keep them in line.

Employment
Ghetto: Streets filled with unemployed; with no money, or transportation to the suburbs, or special skills when they can get there.
Suburbs: Help wanted signs. "Why don't they come to work?"

Local Government
Suburbs: "We can manipulate it."
Ghetto: "It manipulates us."

54

When clergy and laypeople take a conscientious look at prejudice, we might conclude that it is so deep rooted that there is little any one of us can do about it. Blacks struggle with whites, youth with age, men with women over power, influence, and the right to their share of God's world. Such divisions might tempt us to agree with Rudyard Kipling when he wrote "never the twain shall meet."

But we are Christians. We are called to the goal of "one faith, one Lord, one baptism," and we remember that our Lord prayed that we all may be one. In the midst of divisions we sing, "In Christ there is no East or West . . . but one great fellowship of love."

Those of us who have answered God's call to ministry, as well as those who faithfully worship in the churches, would not continue in our faithfulness if we did not believe the love of God could heal the brokenness of divided communities, as well as the divisions among nations. Christ did not say that all persons are created equal but he did say that all are equal in the sight of God and that, in loving us all, God calls us all to be one family. That is the shape of the future.

"Limited World"

They tell us we live in a "limited world."

    Just so much water,
    drink it, waste it, recycle it, drink it again!
    Just so much land,
    more and more people living on less and less!
    Just so much air,
    the world is a ball encased in an air-filled balloon!

And they tell us we are "limited persons."
Each enclosed in definite boundaries of being:

    male or female,
    black or white,
    young or old,
    Jew or Gentile,
    upper-class or under-class,
    bright or dull,
    rich or poor,
    boy or girl.

I believed them,
until I discovered
the power
that breaks limitations.

    Male and female can be fused into one by love.
    Grandparents and children enter each other's world by
        love.
    The prodigal's private life can be invaded by love.
    The barriers of race and color can be breached by love.

The power to break the boundaries,
lies within our selves.

The world is as limitless as is our ability to love.

Thy Will
Be Done on Earth

"Who has not found the heaven below
Will fail of it above.
God's residence is next to mine,
His furniture is love."

—Emily Dickinson, *Poems,* Pt.i, No 100

The Ministry — a Lonely Outpost

As a matter of fact, the clergy are often lonely even before
they enter the profession. A high percentage of us come from
families in which we have been the only child. We have learned
independence and often loneliness from the beginning. These
traits persist in school and in college. We are not joiners, and
many of us have not been a part of team sports. Instead, we tend
to choose lifestyles where our independence can continue. We are

57

apt to be interested in the leadership of clubs or programs. Is it any wonder that when we seek career employment we consider a type of work which allows for independence?

Ministry and leadership of churches is often a one-man or one-woman job. In large measure we make our own decisions, we plan our own schedules, and we perform most of our services on an individual basis. We are not only free from much regulation or supervision, but we are also in a very lonely position.

But there are other reasons which make ministry a "lonely outpost." Most pastors are a part of a church system (called by different names according to the denomination) that is so issue-oriented, as well as program-centered, that the administrators, such as bishops and superintendents, are forced into roles which deny them time to adequately deal with the personel needs of individual pastors. Programs become more important than persons. Projects make more demands than ailing pastors, who are used to solving their own problems by themselves. The forward movement of the institution—the church—takes precedence over the personal needs of many whom it calls to lead. That is rather strange when you stop to think about it, because it is the emotional and spiritual good health of the pastors upon which the church programs and projects depend.

Clergy are called by Paul to create a vocation which has "unity of Spirit" and to have as our objective "one Lord, one faith, one baptism," (Eph. 4:5) Nevertheless, it is our interpretation of the gospels that keeps us separated from the oneness that could overcome our loneliness. The "liberal" pastor does not agree with the "fundamental" one. We are further divided over whether the order of the church service should be highly liturgical or spontaneous and free. We are kept from the unity that might speak to our loneliness when some of us follow a denomination that emphasizes works, and others feel faith is the important part. We are Marthas and Marys, but we do not live in the same house. (Luke 10:40)

Loneliness is not always the fault of the clergy. Too many church members are insensitive to the personal needs of their pastors. Even though pastors might make the effort to bridge the gap between pulpit and pew, not enough laity really accept their pastor as a human individual with emotional, spiritual, and physical needs. One pastor told me:

58

I preach about a sustaining fellowhip;about a brother-hood and sisterhood in the caring spirit of Christ; and I work toward creating small groups for mutual sharing and support, but when such groups are formed, they leave me out.

At least two other causes for loneliness in the ministry can be mentioned. One, there are the clergy who want to make a name for themselves, who want to move to bigger and bigger churches and responsibilities. Often their concern about personal recognition and success defeats the efforts of their peers for caring fellowships.

Two, clergy schedules contribute to loneliness. When secular friends are free on weekends, pastors are working. When pastors are free, perhaps on Mondays, the people with whom they would share recreation are employed. Even when friends may plan social events, they often leave the pastor's family out: "Don't invite the pastor. I wouldn't feel comfortable with him (or her) present."

Finally, ministry is a lonely outpost for other reasons. Pastors live in the world but are not of the world. We busy ourselves on earth, but our citizenship is in heaven. We obey the established laws, but in our own lives we go far beyond what those laws require. We may be hired by churches but we are really servants of the Lord.

This immersion in life but separation from it confronts us with many spiritual decisions.

When local self-interest on the part of a visionless church board protects a plush endowment instead of investing funds in missions, do we campaign for a new board or do we take more drastic measures? What stand do we have when our white membership refuses to welcome blacks? How do we protest when money is spent for cosmetic building improvements to the detriment of more support for the Sunday School? When social programs to help refugees are voted down, do we just express our disappointment or do we act more decisively?

In many ways, pastors have to stand for unpopular causes. In so doing, we may be lonely but we are not alone! We have courage, strength and purpose the world knows not of. We stand in the tradition of the prophets. We are in the company of a great cloud of witnesses. We are not really lonely!

Women in the Pulpit

A female critic of this review of ministry asked why I include a special section on women. She pointed out that women do not want to be seen as special cases. It should automatically be assumed that there are women ministers, so why give them a special heading?

The fact is, however, that women pastors are news today. In one large metropolitan area having 155 churches of just one denomination, there are only ten full-time women pastors. (There are a few other women who have been ordained, but they are either serving as co-pastors with their husbands or lead a church only on a half-time basis.

The history of the church does not include many women in the clergy role. Males have provided leadership for centuries, with women as helpers. But now that's changing. Today, more and more women are graduating from the nation's seminaries and are seeking roles as pastors. Although job placement is very difficult at present, many congregations are being slowly introduced to new styles of ministry that include women.

Churches are employing couples as co-pastors. Both are ordained and share equally in all aspects of ministry: preaching, calling, counseling, conducting weddings and funerals, and administering Holy Communion.

As more women are being ordained, they are bringing new insights to the gospel. They are challenging the old sexist language that is found throughout scripture as well as in hymns. They are expanding concepts of theology because of their feminine point of view on life. They are offering new styles of leadership. Congregations that have called women have experienced new growth and new depths of spiritual appreciation.

Women are skilled at putting people in touch with people. They are creators of networks for mutual help. Although generalizations are dangerous, many women pastors refrain from "using" groups as do some men; women see the group as solely for its own ends, not theirs.

The road to acceptance of women in the pulpit has many barriers. One is the matter of visibility. Women broke the exclusion barrier as commentators on TV when a few courageous stations made their talents visible. The public became educated, and more and more women appeared on the screen. With more women working as executives in business, occupying influential political offices nationwide, and being leaders in the media, there will be more women ministers.

It may be an unwarranted generalization, but it seems as though women are not as cutthroat competitors as men. They seem more interested in doing their work with a sense of fresh creativity. They seem to have more sensitivity to human growth.

It would appear, at least now, that many women do not aspire to be the boss. However, this may be due to the fact that there are not enough women in prominent positions who could aid and abet a colleague who hopes for such a role.

Women in leadership are an encouragement to all women to anticipate great opportunities. The church that considers a woman as pastor or co-pastor is giving a clear message of recognition to every woman in that parish, and new life may certainly result. On the other hand, many congregations have lost talented and capable women as new members because their pulpit committees hung a "No Woman Wanted" sign out, when they considered refilling their pulpits.

The presence of women pastors is news! That is bound to change, for the better, the traditional male-dominated image of ministry.

Stress and Burn-out

A significant occupational hazard for clergy is that time when emotional, physical, and even spiritual powers are drained, when enthusiasm for the parish drops to a low ebb and the pastor feels overcome by stress. A common name for such a situation is burn-out.

Stress and burn-out happen to pastors for several reasons, one of which is worry over inadequate pay.

Ministry attracts men and women who are more motivated by their sense of call than by the size of salary, but when their families grow and they face financial demands of improved education for their children or added responsibility for aging relatives, the threat of stress arises. Relatively low pay is common to most small churches, even though they may be supported by the denomination. The low standard of living plus high expectancy of performance puts many a pastor in a financial and emotional bind. In spite of prayers, God does not always guarantee us a level of income that we would like, so stress takes its toll on families as well as pastor's careers.

Another prevalent cause for occupational strain arises from the differences in the pastor's idea of success and the expectation of the congregation. Clergy interpret achievement in terms of effective personal counseling, superior preaching, care of the sick and shut-ins, as well as fulfilling a myriad of community responsibilities. On the other hand, congregations often expect the pastor to bring many new members into an old church, revive the Sunday School, and not antagonize the various clusters of political loyalties within the parish. Pastors want to be pastors. Congregations want us to be administrators who will be successful in terms of numbers as well as income. Some clergy have the wisdom of Solomon to deal with expectations that can be impossible. Some others find the stress burning out their spirit.

Exorbitant demands upon a pastor's time can also hamper a clergyperson's effectiveness and enthusiasm for parish work. Inner city clergy are often barraged with a constant stream of needy folks at the church or parsonage door.

"How can I help so many?" one pastor asks," Their urgent pleas even disturb my sleep at night."

Of course, suburban and rural ministers face overload too, often in the area of personal and family counseling.

"The emotional drain of hours and hours of counseling, on top of my other duties, taxes my faith," reports one man, "I need more time than the parish will allow just to recharge my spiritual batteries."

Another reason for clergy burn-out is the conflict that can arise between a conscientious pastor and a layperson who wants to make all the decisions about life in the parish. (I suggest an example of this and its expected consequences in a story in this book titled "Thank You, My Enemy.")

Congregations, too, can be a cause for clergy burn-out. In fact, few parishioners know how debilitating it can be for a pastor to face such constant comments as, "We've never done it that way before" or "That won't work" or "I've done my part.; let someone else do it." People who take such attitudes do not seem to realize how negative they sound and how depressing their apathy appears. Unfortunately, their frame of mind is not new. The writer of the Book of Revelation complained of a parish that was neither hot nor cold, so that one felt like spitting it out of one's mouth (Rev. 3:15).

Overloaded work schedules, conflict over parish authority, depression brought on by congregational apathy, differences between congregation and pastor over job expectancies and salary levels—all these and more can result in discouragement, loss of spirit and burn-out. An example of this is prophet Elijah (1 Kings 17—18).

One of the most dedicated prophets, Elijah began his ministry relatively unknown. Great accomplishments of faith occurred, only to be succeeded by times of discouragement. At one point, Elijah was so depressed and burned-out that he was ready to give up and even asked for death. But Elijah had more divine resources than he knew, as is the case with the modern pastor.

God met Elijah in the midst of his dejection. Through an angel, God provided food. Through a widow's dying son, God reminded Elijah of his spiritual powers. Through Elijah's awareness of God's still, small voice, God reawakened his belief. Through an assignment to a new career in a different place, God lifted Elijah out of depression.

The process by which Elijah overcame burn-out suggests a cure for stress today: proper nourishment, rest and relaxation, reawakening of faith, a perspective about ministry, or a new location for service.

To Be or Not to Be a Minister

There are predictable crises in the life of every pastor—the trauma of taking a different life road than our friends as we choose the unusual career of ministry, incidents during the pastoral years which test our faith about being professional Christians, and sometimes having to decide whether to stay in or actually leave the church. Indeed, knowing why people enter or leave gives helpful perspective on the unseen spiritual battles of the profession.

1. *Why Men and Women Enter the Ministry*
"I felt the Call of God."

"When I was in high school, Rev. Harris had a great influence on me. A number of us from his church are now pastors."

"My father was a minister. I can tell you coming from a minister's family has sure helped me move upward in the denomination, faster than other men my same age. He taught me how to handle power in the church."

"One night when I was young, I lay on top of our outhouse, impressed by the wonder of the stars. I stayed there for hours. I felt so near to God I knew the ministry was for me."

"I felt I needed to serve some cause greater than myself."

"Like Jane Addams, I was moved by seeing how poor people live. My parents had lots of money and wanted me to be a lawyer, but I have been happy working through the church to change a lousy social system."

"My specialty is children, and how we can teach them about the Bible and Jesus as they are growing up."

"I wanted to change society and the world, and felt the church had the chance of bringing that about."

2. *The Rewards of Being in the Ministry*
"Seeing the town political crook attending church and really meaning it."

"Realizing you can make a mistake as a pastor and still be accepted and loved."

"Ministry has allowed me to have friends who have been leaders in slum clearance and programs for employment and minorities. Working with business executives who give their influence and expertise to such projects has been rewarding."

"When you find people trust you with the most important decision of their lives."

"Experiencing my own salvation."

"One of the greatest rewards of my ministry has been to see inexperienced men or women assume jobs in the church, grow in them, and become leaders in their own right in other church programs. I see myself as an enabler."

"A reward for me is to have shared a painful crisis with a family in which the faith of all of us has been challenged, and then to see those involved find new foundations of faith."

"In the middle years of my pastorate, I slipped into a long period of depression. It was a layman who helped me the most. I will never forget him. He taught me a lot about forgiveness and sacrificial love."

"My greatest joy is when I see someone really turned on by new faith. I have seen people changed overnight by Christ, divorces given up, hatreds overcome, purposeless lives renewed by the Spirit."

3. *The Greatest Difficulties of the Role of Pastor, As Pastors See Them*

"Finding time to be with one's family!"

"Dealing with a parishioner who uses the church as his own small kingdom, that is, the member who wants to be the 'king of the hill.'"

"In my church, I'm always called 'Pastor.' I appreciate the title, but when my best friends in the church use it I feel it puts a gulf between us. I feel as if they always see me as an official separated from them"

"The need to be both pastor and prophet is difficult for me. I see the need to comfort the afflicted and also to afflict the comfortable. Really, doing that takes a lot of doing!"

"Getting out to do jobs I don't like to do, such as calling or raising money."

"Having a more liberal theology than my church will accept."

"A Bible-pounding, faith-healing group developed in my parish because of one family's agitation. I tried to give them freedom to speak, but they did not do the same for me. It was a hair-raising year for that congregation before the family left to join another church."

"In one of my churches, I got into an argument over policies. In retaliation, the treasurer always delayed my paycheck, a parishioner would secretly listen outside of my office door to my

65

counseling sessions, and someone was always going through my wastebasket. A church member who lived across the street from our parsonage circulated daily news of what my wife was doing."

When a Pastor Leaves a Church

There will be more people in church on the day a new minister preaches his or her first sermon than there may be for several years afterwards. But when a pastor leaves, the attendance is much less predictable. It depends on whether the pastor is (1) fired or dismissed, (2) retires, (3) leaves for a different occupation, or (4) moves to another parish.

1. Dismissing or asking a pastor to resign is never a pleasant task. By the time such action is necessary the feelings throughout the church may become so frayed that unreasonable things may happen. A congregation sued its pastor because they felt he had not earned months of salary that had already been paid. Another parish instituted a campaign of silence during which no one spoke to the pastor as a way of encouraging him to leave. Of course, poison-pen letters are not unexpected in such situations either. On the other hand, one pastor was so emotionally upset with conflict over his ministry and requested resignation that he purposely damaged the utilities of the parsonage and made it look accidental. (Such illustrations are, of course, the exceptions.)

When emotions of anger and distrust run high, with a final separation inevitable, it is unfortunate that it takes some months for a minister to find a new parish. But even during the difficult time, I am convinced that the burden of conciliation lies more with the pastor than with the parishioners, whatever the circumstances. We are called by our Lord to be reconcilers. We are those who preach forgiveness in His name.

Although it is not uncommon to hear some pastors continue to malign former church members, such unresolved bitterness may say more about the lack of Christian maturity of the pastor than about the problem of the parish.

2. Retirement for the clergy is different from that of a union member or a businessman or woman. Clergy do not have to observe a mandatory retirement age; in fact, some work up to

and through their seventies, as long as they have good health and can find small congregations which do not need long hours or have heavy schedules. Nor is retirement the traumatic disruption of a clergyperson's lifestyle. Much of a pastor's career is spent with books, in study, family counseling, and learning to adjust to various age levels. The pastor has known church members of the senior years, so it is comparatively easy to move into them on a personal basis.

The matter of finances is always a consideration, but for the clergy who have always received relatively low pay, the threat of poverty is mitigated by few material expectancies. Clergy do not live for things. Their needs are generally less than other people's. Indeed, a fund for retired pastors, of which I happen to be a part, has a difficult time in actually finding retired clergy who are in financial need. Retired clergy are fine examples of the joy of the simpler life as well as the security represented by genuine values instead of material things.

3. When a pastor loses faith in the church and turns to a different career, the extent to which ministry is a specialized job becomes apparent. Knowledge of church history, Christian education, the Old Testament, the life of Jesus, and theology are not good preparations for a job in business. On the other hand, experience in working with all kinds of people is good background for sales jobs, and years of counseling can be developed into a new career as a marriage counselor or professional therapist. Some pastors, utilizing the experience of their own tours to the Holy Land, become travel guides. Others become administrators of human-service institutions such as rest homes and health care centers. A number become teachers or personnel directors.

Some clergy leave the church because they become frustrated with the institution, finding it too slow in getting things done or too timid in preaching the faith. Sometimes they become frustrated because the congregation does not take the faith seriously enough.

4. Leaving a church for another parish is like losing a very dear relative. Years and years of close friendships suddenly are broken. The security of loving and being loved is interrupted without real hope of continuation, for when a minister leaves a parish it is professional courtesy to turn over all relationship with parishioners to the incoming pastor. Going back for weddings or

special family occasions is not good professional conduct. Leaving a long pastorate is an emotional experience, not unlike losing a part of one's personal life.

I have served several churches, each for a period of fourteen years. Over those long pastorates many deep and abiding friendships were established, confidences were shared, tears and laughter known, and trust developed. Yet when I left each parish, I had to leave all of that behind as a new spiritual leader took my place. Letters and holiday cards have partially filled my yearning to know how life has been for such friends, but the direct involvement I used to have with them is out of the question. As I have not moved far away from former parishes, I have partially allayed my loneliness by occasionally going back to those communities and driving by the homes of church members I formerly knew so well. Each house brings a different memory: a wedding, a secret sin, a tragedy, a birth, a courageous battle with illness, a newfound faith, a changed life, a nobility of age, and so much more.

Though I cannot actively continue those friendships, every one of them stands out clearly in my mind and heart, and my present ministry is constantly shaped by the Spirit I experienced in my former parishes.

. . . .

We make a mistake if we conclude that the state of the church depends entirely on the presence of the professional clergy. We must always remember that the people to whom Christ entrusted the future of his church were fishermen—in every sense of the word, laypersons.

The Layperson Is a Minister, Too

Conscientious pastors are aware of the necessity, both for their own sake as well as for the benefit of their congregation, to continue to improve their skills through all the years of ministry.

We always need to keep abreast of new methods for church growth and current insights into more effective counseling. We need an ever deeper awareness of our spiritual roles as clergy.

Some churches demand and set set aside several weeks during the year, in addition to vacation time, for their pastors to continue their education.

So it was that I attended summer school classes on numerous occasions at a New York City school of theology.

As part of my assignments, I attended different churches to observe their styles of worship. One Sunday, I chose a famous Manhattan cathedral and looked forward to hearing its well-known preacher. But he was not the pastor who impressed me. Instead, when the service was over and I was preparing to leave, an elderly lady whom I had noticed sitting in a nearby pew made it a point to speak to me.

"I hope you enjoyed the music and sermon this morning," she said.

"Yes, thank you, I did," I replied.

"This is my church," she continued. "I used to be a missionary in Turkey, but I'm retired now and keep active here. You're always welcome; I hope you come again."

Such a friendly introduction led to several moments of good conversation.

It was not so much the words she used as the way she spoke which I remember. She seemed to have a genuine sincerity. She did not give me the impression of being a "soul-saver" who was anxious to convert me. Rather, I felt she deeply cared for people and wanted to reach out, even to a stranger.

I have long forgotten the message of the pastor, but I still recall the friendly, personal concern of that woman. A missionary and an older church member, she could have been aloof and indifferent, as so many church members can be. Instead, she extended herself to me, a much younger, transient visitor. (A caring greeting from a regular member can often do more to bring new people into the congregation than the pastor's sermon. People want and need to be loved.)

I want to remind every reader of this book that caring for people, serving them, accepting them, forgiving them, and sharing life fully with them in the spirit of Jesus Christ is doing the will of God.

As you worship in your church, don't allow the distance of your pew from the pulpit, or even the height of the pulpit, to be a sign that you are unequal to your pastor in the work of God. I know many parishioners who surpass me in the practice of their religious beliefs.

When you sit in your pew before your pastor, don't despair because you have not had as much training in the faith as he or she. Being able to love in the spirit of Jesus Christ does not depend upon intellect. With all of their seminary courses and academic degrees, no pastor is nearer to God than the layperson who sincerely believes in the Lord.

The Bible is not a volume of academic facts but rather a book about values and morals. The great question of life is not how much you know but what kind of values and morals you stand for. As you request membership, your church will not ask you, "How intelligent are you?" but it may well ask, "Do you believe in Jesus Christ, and will you seek to become one of his faithful disciples?"

I want to say to every layperson: You have as much a right to do God's will as the so-called professional clergy. Do not count yourself ill-prepared just because you do not have as much education or social position. If a formal education is the key to understanding God's will, then our Lord would have entrusted the future of his ministry to the educated Jewish rabbis of his day.

Every pastor can tell of times and circumstances when a layperson became an outstanding example of what it means to be a Christian.

"Sweetheart"

My first meeting with the Tuckers was a memorable one. I had driven my car into the driveway of their small, dilapidated frame cottage on the outskirts of town. As I walked up their sidewalk, I thought I saw a woman peeking from behind the curtains of the front window.

I was greeted at the door by Mr. Tucker. However, when I entered I found no woman around. Mr. Tucker immediately volunteered:

70

"You will have to excuse my sweetheart. She is afraid of strangers. You see, she is not well. She has been in the hospital any number of times."

Just then, a pale, emaciated woman appeared in the hall doorway. She just stood rather uncertainly, apparently unable to make up her mind whether to join us or not. After a long hesitation, she began to count:

"One, two, three, four, five, six," and continued up to fifteen.

"I have to count my swallows," she explained, then asked, looking suspiciously at me,"Who are you?"

"This is the pastor," Mr. Tucker interrupted. "It's all right, sweetheart. Come and sit with me on the sofa."

She shuffled into the room, holding her stomach as if in much pain.

"I have stones in here," she complained. "I don't sleep at night. Are you the cause of that?"

I was surprised by her question and was groping for an answer when her husband interceded.

"Grace has been sick a long time. I can't leave her, you know. Not left her for five years now . . . Have a workbench in the basement. Thank God for that . . . I spend a lot of time there . . . I get out for groceries, that's all."

"Can she help herself in any way?" I asked.

"No," he replied, "We used to go to church every Sunday, but about ten years ago she began to suspect the neighbors were talking about her, so we stopped going out. It got worse and I got her into a hospital, but they didn't do much for her. Since then, she's been out and in different places."

As he spoke, I had a chance to look around the room. The wallpaper was a faded, dull brown color. The furniture was old and well worn. The soiled curtains were closely drawn so as to keep out as much sunlight as possible. Her husband went on to explain their lives in greater detail.

Apparently his wife spent most of her time in the bedroom. She had given up cleaning the house many years ago, so he had become the housekeeper. She had no interest in anything, not even TV, but sometimes looked at pictures in a magazine. She just sat and stared into the distance most of the time. She was suspicious of everyone; so the church people no longer stopped by to call, and no other visitors ever came to see her.

After an hour of visiting, I told Mr. Tucker I had to leave, but made a promise to myself to return for more of their story.

Later I stopped at the home a number of times. One call seemed specially significant in retrospect.

The three of us were sitting in the darkened living room. Mrs. Tucker was on the sofa. She was bent over with her chin in her hands, perhaps counting the "stones" in her stomach. She wore an old, plain, black dress. Her cloth slippers were broken out at both the toes and the heels. Her eyes were sunken spots in a sallow face that seemed contorted by some inner evil spirits. She appeared to be a burden even to herself. As I carefully watched her, I wondered which would take her first, death or the closed ward of another hospital.

Across the room sat Mr. Tucker. I thought he must have been about seventy, but he seemed relatively young. He had on a clean white shirt and rather well-pressed slacks. His shoes were old-fashioned, but cared for. He looked at me in a direct, friendly manner.

I could not help reflecting on his future. How would he face the remaining years of his own life with such a helpless, pathetic invalid? How much longer could he continue to care for a woman who could do nothing to help herself? What gave him the inner strength to keep going?

Suddenly, Mrs. Tucker began to count again, at the same time looking at me with a wild, suspicious expression. Quickly, her husband got up, walked across the room and put his arm around her shoulder in a protective way.

"It's all right," he said patiently. "Don't worry. This man is not going to take you away. We've been through this before. You'll be well again, just like the girl I married. Isn't that so, sweetheart?"

"Sweetheart!" I don't think she ever heard the word. But I heard it! Yes, I heard it: a husband using an endearing term to reach down into the darkened mind of a sick woman. I heard a man descend into his wife's hell to redeem her through love.

It has been a long time since that visit. The woman passed away some months afterward; her husband became ill with terminal cancer and lived only a few years longer. But I still hear that devoted man calling his wife "Sweetheart."

Let the social workers say he undermined her by overindulgence. But where were they when he began coping with her in the only way he knew? Let the psychiatrists observe that it was a dishonest kind of affection. Where were they when she was dismissed time and again from hospitals without any cure?

It may be easy to judge this man and say, "He should have done it differently." The fact of the matter is that he did what he thought best, and though he might not have met professional standards, he met a deeper level of commitment; he loved without counting the cost.

Indeed, Mr. Tucker, a layperson, has been a lasting sermon to me; his actions have been a more memorable example of the Christian faith.

"Here was a man," I have reflected, "who did more than recite the Apostle's Creed. In one sense he lived it. He descended into the hell of his wife's existence in an effort to bring her back to life."

How many times parishioners, by their practice of the faith, teach us pastors about the love of Christ.

. . . .

We pastors and laypersons are always revealing the extent of our faith by the way we live. "You yourselves are our letter of recommendation," wrote Paul, ". . . to be known and read of all men." (2 Cor. 3:2)

Each one of us either supports or undermines our families and our world by the choices which direct our lives. We are either good examples or poor examples to all those who know us, affecting them for good or evil.

For example, consider what we do with our bodies. The way we use them, the purposes for which we expend them, and the value we place upon them reveal our understanding of the meaning of life and our relationship with God—namely, our theology.

"Her Body and Her Theology"

She fulfilled her body;
      realizing one of the purposes of womanhood,
      bringing forth children in love,
      continuing the heritage of her parents,
      glorifying the divine grace of motherhood.

She sold her body;
      to men who enjoyed themselves,
      and filled her purse,
      emptying themselves of respect for God's creation,
      and filling her with a false sense of values.

She gave her body in service;
      not in union but in ministration,
      (washing, nursing and healing the sick)
      'til it aged and wore out before its time,
      but gave off an aura of peace and love.

She loaned her body for adventure;
      changing many partners on the surface of life,
      living like a bouquet of flowers,
      which, having no roots,
      faded, and was soon thrown away.

She dedicated her body to her family;
      rising up while it was yet night,
      to provide food for her household.
      Integrity and character were her clothing.
      Her children grew up to call her blessed,
      she and her husband were "known in the gates."

She saved her body for herself;
    enshrouding it with frigid self-denials,
    keeping it as a walled castle,
    inviolate and pristine chaste.
    Even the ground around her grave
    was as cold and flowerless as her life.

She cherished her body;
    developing the health of her figure,
    cultivating her feelings of sensuality,
    sharing herself in sacred love with her man,
    enjoying the mystical meanings of her sex,
    which God had created and called good.

A woman's body . . . fulfilled, saved, given, sold,
    expended, loaned, dedicated, cherished.

How she lives is a testament to her theology!

Give Us
This Day
Our Daily Bread

"Alas for the unhappy man that is called to stand in the pulpit, and not give the bread of life."

—Emerson: Address to the Senior Class in Divinity College, Cambridge, July 15, 1838.

The Word As "Bread"

The phrase "Give us this day our daily bread," from the Lord's Prayer is usually associated with the prayer for food. We ask that we always have something to eat.

But a second look reveals a far deeper meaning. The word "bread" may also be pointing us to companionship with God and with Jesus Christ, as the real nourishment.

"Jesus then said to them, 'Truly, truly, I say to you, it was not Moses who gave you the bread from heaven; my Father gives you the true bread from heaven. For the bread of God is that which comes down from heaven, and gives life to the world.' They said to him, 'Lord, give us this bread always.' Jesus said to them, 'I am the bread of life; he who comes to me shall not hunger, and he who believes in me shall never thirst.'" (John 6:32-35)

So it is the bread of life that we also pray for in the Lord's Prayer. It is not just bread for our stomachs but bread for our souls, not bread which comes from man but bread which comes from heaven, not nourishment at the world's hand but sustenance from God's hand.

The Power of Scripture

Several years ago my daughter was in a violent traffic accident. A giant semi loaded with gravel ran a red light at high speed and smashed into the side of her small car. Needless to say, she was seriously injured. Many months of hospitalization followed, during which she received skilled care from various kinds of doctors.

At first her recovery seemed uncertain, but as the days and weeks wore on she regained her will to live. Her broken bones seemed to mend with unusual speed, and her return to a full life finally became assured. In fact, her injured body and severe internal problems responded to the specialists far more quickly than any of the doctors had predicted.

An explanation did not appear until many weeks after she finally returned home for recuperation.

"I am convinced that the main reason I am alive today," she explained, "is because of the new presence of God in my life. I am thankful for the help of my doctors, to be sure, but it was my thoughts of God which really gave me the support I needed."

I found it unusual to hear her speak in such religious terms. As a growing young woman she had taked an interest in Christian Science, but she had not taken it seriously. Nor had she ever attended church much, as the children of many pastors are likely to do. In fact, I never thought that the Bible or faith meant anything to her at all. When she stated that God had been an important help, I encouraged her to tell me more.

"I need to explain," she added, "that I had many terrible nights in the hospital. I felt like giving up a number of times. You remember that I could not even move my head for weeks. The constant pain was awful. But in the midst of it all, a strange comfort occasionally came to me. At first I thought it was the power of my drugs, but then I discovered that it was the power of God."

I could hardly believe what my daughter was saying—this child who had never thought about the church and who, I suspected, knew even less about the Bible. Naturally, I asked her to explain what she was saying.

"I cannot remember what I learned in Sunday school," she admitted, "nor can I recall a lot that you preached about. But you were the minister as well as my father, and an occasional Bible passage stuck in my mind. In fact, I guess I remember more than I thought, for when things looked the blackest I found myself repeating bits and pieces of the Bible."

"Such as?" I interrupted.

"Yes," she continued, "such as 'You shall walk and not faint,' and 'God is the strength of my life,' and 'Fear not, I am with you, I will give you aid.' I could not find the strength to think of more than short passages such as these. But whenever I thought of them, I regained the will to live. I felt God was helping me. I cannot tell you how, I just knew it."

"Did you ever pray for your recovery?" I asked.

"Not at first," she replied. "As I look back upon it now, I was too emotionally drained to pray. My body was broken; I guess my spirit was broken too. I just did not have the spiritual power to pray. But as I began to get better, I found the strength to think more and more about those verses from the Bible. I guess they helped me more than anything. They seemed like anchors in the physical storm I was passing through."

My daughter's answer to my question about prayer intrigued me. What is prayer? Even in the critical first hours of her injury, I had not prayed. That is, I had not been on my knees. I had not read the Bible, nor had I stood beside her bed and uttered words of appeal to God. Somehow I thought that would be wrong. I knew God cared; I knew God was all-powerful; I knew God wanted people to be well, including my daughter.; I knew conscientious trained doctors and nurses would meet her needs. My spiritual being moved me to express thanksgiving that she was alive. I would do all I could to help her get well, but I did not ask God for any special attention. God would do what God thought best—I had no doubt of that. I had absolute trust. Perhaps that in itself is a prayer.

In retrospect, my daughter's reliance on scripture passages in the midst of her suffering and my more seasoned adult faith reveal how God works among us all. Being a new and youthful traveler upon the Way, my daughter needed roadsigns to show her the path to faith. Having traveled longer on the highway, I could keep the path without resorting to the signposts. In both cases, God came to us, as God can come to everybody, and that made all the difference.

"Mother"

Some time ago, a friend of mine named Jack asked me to get a leather-bound Bible for him. He said he would like to have the word "Mother" inscribed on the cover in gold.

When the book arrived, I went to his house to deliver it. But as I drove there, I kept wondering why he wanted a Bible. He had never impressed me as being a religious person, and I couldn't remember his ever attending church. I felt he was part of that large segment of American men who drink beer in the kitchen on Saturday night, sleep late on Sunday, and never think of religion.

I got to the place at about two in the afternoon, with the idea of leaving the Bible package on the front porch. I was surprised to find Jack answering the doorbell.

"Yeah, Rev, I'm here," he explained. "Had an accident at the plant. Damned piece of machinery fell on my foot. Damned near killed me. Company doc sent me to the hospital. Been there a couple of days. Just got back."

I was still standing in the doorway when he added, "Say, come in, will ya? I got somethin' on my mind."

I found the home very plain. The living room furniture appeared well worn and old. There was a faded picture of Niagara Falls on the wall and some fake flowers in a vase on the TV.

Newspapers and magazines were piled on the floor next to an overstuffed sofa.

"It's about my son, Rev," he continued when we had settled into two well used easy chairs.

"Ya see, he's signed up for a hitch in the army. Leaving soon. Thursday, to be exact. I don't know what I'm gonna do with him away. He's my boy. Been camping together since he was a little tyke. Been huntin' and fishin' too—for years. That's his gun there on the wall. I'm gonna miss him all right. It's sure gonna be lonesome around' here."

He pulled a large handkerchief from his pocket and wiped his eyes, then continued:

"Mary, that's my wife, ya know. She's a basket case. I wish ya could speak to her. She needs some of that religious stuff of yours. I'm kinda upset, too."

I wanted to tell my friend it would be all right if he cried, that I might cry too, if I were in his shoes. Then the front door opened, and in walked a tall, well-built, athletic-looking young man.

"This here's Bill," Jack said. "Bill, meet the Rev."

Bill gave me a strong, warm handshake.

"Glad to meet ya," he said. "Come to get some papers. I'm selling my bike. Won't need it in the Army. See ya." He bounded up the stairs, three at a time, to the bedroom above.

"Yeah, that's my boy," Jack exclaimed when Bill was out of sight. "I'm gonna miss him. He's all I got."

I had just stopped off to deliver a book. Instead, I found myself in the midst of a personal crisis, a father and son facing their first real separation. What was my responsibility? How could I help the older man through his worry and fear of the separation? How could I support the son, if he needed support? I was struggling with this when suddenly I thought of the Bible package. "What about the Bible?" I said to myself. "The father is so upset, he is not thinking of why I came." So I suggested:

"I hope the Bible is the kind you wanted."

"Yeah," Jack replied. "I got it for Bill. He wants to give it to his mother before he goes. Hey, Bill," he yelled, "The Rev brought your Bible."

"O.K., O.K.," came Bill's voice from upstairs. "I'll be right down."

In a moment he bounded down the stairs and into the living room. At the same time, I heard a back door bang.

"I'm home," someone shouted. "Who's here? I seen a car in the driveway."

"That must be his wife," I reflected, as I heard her setting some packages on the kitchen table. Then she joined us.

"Hello," she said, "I'm Mary. Would you all like a cup of coffee?"

I replied that I had just finished lunch, when Bill saved my further apologies by interrupting: "Hey, Ma. Here's a book I got for ya." He held out the package with pride.

"What kind of book is it?" she asked.

"Open it," Bill continued anxiously. "Open it."

Mary began to unwrap the package carefully. She seemed curious about it, as if unsure whether to expect a joke or a gift. When part of the leather cover appeared, she almost stopped. Then she took off the rest of the wrapping paper and saw the word "Mother." For an instant, I did not know what was going to happen. She clutched the Bible to her breast, looked at Bill and Jack, and then, without warning, burst into tears. Almost dropping the book, but being careful to lay it on the floor before she got up, she fled to the kitchen. I could hear her sobbing there. Bill turned to his father.

"What's the trouble?" he asked.

No one moved. Each of us was alone with his own thoughts. It was several moments before she came back.

"I'm sorry," she explained. "I've never had a Bible before in my whole life. I never dreamed Bill would do such a thing. You know, he's going away soon. Jack and I will be all by ourselves for the first time. It's going to be different without our boy."

I had just stopped to deliver a Bible, but I found myself in the midst of an experience which three people would probably remember for the rest of their lives. Suddenly I thought, "What this family needs is to talk more about what is going on."

"I feel we need some time together now," I suggested. "Mary, why don't you get that coffee you talked about."

Soon we were all sharing memories and laughs. Jack told of the time he and Bill shot two skunks, which backfired on them. Bill reported that he got more for his bike than he had thought he would. Mary thanked Bill over and over for the Bible, as she kept looking at it with reverence.

As I watched the sharing, I felt we had moved to a deeper relationship in which prayer could play a part.

"Bill is going into an unknown future," I explained. "All of us are concerned about that, as Bill is. I believe that prayer is a way of sorting out our lives, a way of bringing to mind those things we feel are important. Prayer is also a way of discovering that God shares our fears and anxieties, as well as our love for each other. Would you like me to share in prayer with you while I'm here?"

No one replied to my suggestion, but I noticed that all heads were bowed. After a moment of silence, I prayed that Bill might find military life would help him grow phyically and mentally. I prayed that God would be with Mary and Jack as they discovered new meanings in each other's lives while living alone together. And I prayed that each of us might be able to turn to the Bible for faith and direction. Then I suggested that all of us share in the Lord's Prayer.

After ending the prayer, I purposely kept my eyes closed for a moment, for I could hear Jack and Mary weeping. When I looked up, Jack was putting his handkerchief back in his pocket.

"Thanks, Rev, " he said.

Mary covered up her emotion by going to the kitchen for more coffee.

When we began talking again, I noticed it was on a very different level from before. Now we began talking about caring for each other and how much family love meant. Bill thanked his parents for all that they had done for him, which brought more moist eyes. Mary moved to sit beside her husband on the couch and held his hand. Jack looked out of the window to avoid exposing more of his feelings.

After a short while, I got up to leave. Mary thanked me for bringing the Bible. Bill said he would write when he received his assignment, so that the church would know. But the most surprising comment was from Jack, who revealed an entirely new attitude toward God as well as the church when he said, "Rev, when you talk to your God in church on Sunday, will you remind him of Bill and Mary and me?"

On Using the Bible

As the preceding stories suggest, the Bible is in fact a great source of spiritual nourishment, restored health, and peace of mind. But it would be unfair to not also observe that the Bible, as every clergyperson knows, can be a source of serious controversy even among those who are the most ardent believers in Jesus Christ and in God.

Even though our Lord calls all who follow him to become one in spirit, the fact remains that churches, denominations, seminaries, pastors, and laypersons are often deeply divided in their understanding of the will of God as revealed in the sacred book. Indeed, the nation's press continually reports the divisions within ecclesiastical bodies over points of belief that arise out of different interpretations of the Scriptures.

As pastors trained in understanding the Bible, we need to remind ourselves that we study and interpret out of our own human frailty and prejudices, no matter how we may try to do otherwise. The truth we claim seems dependent upon our relationship with God as revealed to us through the Holy Spirit. It is not unfair to state that some pastors have more of Christ in their hearts than others, that some preachers comprehend the mysteries of the Bible better than others, and that all who would seek the truth of the Bible-Word must do so subject to the constant correcting and inspring power of the Holy Spirit.

In short, we read the Bible according to how the Spirit has dealt with us.

Some of us take the phrases and sentences literally. We see every part as being the result of God's actual dictation. We do not question any piece for fear of bringing the whole work into question.

Others of us see the Bible as an unfolding drama of the understanding of God. We read that God was first thought of as a giant walking in the Garden of Eden. Later, God appeared as a power that supported God's people in their battles against their enemies. Still later, God seems more concerned with justice and mercy. Finally, in the New Testament, God is portrayed as one who forgives and who loves everybody—bearing all things, hoping all things, and enduring all things.

Reading and interpreting the word of God is a serious responsibility. This is perhaps one of the reasons why there are so many different understandings of what sacred scripture is trying to say to us in our time. Many pastors feel called to preach the social reform theme of the Bible. Others conclude that it is more important to change the individual. (Let the world be changed, Lord, beginning with me.) Some of us are called "conservative," some "liberal." Some are authoritarian, and some are conscious of the rights of every person. Our varieties of souls lead to myriad interpretations of the word. With the world teeming with thousands and thousands of concerns, God needs more than one human voice to interpret the full truth of the purpose and plan for salvation.

Having referred to the multiple choices that we have in testifying to the word as revealed in the Bible, we must add that most pastors probably grieve over the fact that, although the Bible is such a popular book and is so well distributed, it is little read.

Some years ago I received word from a maiden aunt that she was at last sending me a prized copy of an old family Bible. In due time it arrived—a large wooden box insured for quite a sum. I opened it with great anticipation. It was a sizeable volume, the front pages of which contained some of the family's genealogy. As I thoughtfully turned the illustrated pages, I was struck with the obvious fact that it had never been used! Alas, every pastor can tell such a story. Perhaps the differences in interpretation are not so important after all. God must want us to read the word! God will supply the Spirit to guide our understanding.

The Mysterious Word

Visit any church, on any Sunday morning, in any area of the country, with any minister conducting worship, and these are the people you will may sharing in the service:

an old man who can't hear but who comes out of
a lifelong habit;
a few students sitting together;
several men, whose wives have made them attend;
a number of complete strangers, looking around;
several persons who are wondering if the
church really has any answers for their lives;
a man or woman who has been told he or she faces
a life-threatening illness;
a young couple who are attending their first service;
a mixed-up teen-ager with a parent;
several persons who are critical of the sermons
but who attend out of loyalty to their church;
a few couples who, as members of a faith-growth group,
are finding new meanings in their marriages;
more than one or two individuals, men as well as
women, who are struggling with alcohol;
a small core of folks for whom the service is a
deep spiritual experience;
many who are aware that attendance challenges
their week's behavior and who are uneasy
when "sin" is mentioned;
a faithful few who have known the pain of
repentance, the release of confession and
the joy of a new life.

What mysterious power brings modern persons to hear ancient truths? Why do space-minded people of a scientific age seek healing from tribal stories and mystics of a remote time?

The Lord said to me, "Gather the people to me, that I may let them hear my words, so that they may learn to fear me all the days that they live upon the earth, and that they may teach their children so"(Deut. 4:10).

Forgive Us
Our Sins

"'Tis easier work if we begin
    To fear the Lord betimes;
While sinners that grow old in sin
    Are hardened in their crimes."

—Isaac Watts, "Advantages of Early Religion," Circa 1700.

A Heritage in Need of Grace

To write about the sins of the clergy is not to say anything new. As a matter of fact, if you are curious about the sins of religious leaders, read your Bible again.

Jacob lied to his father and then stole his brother Esau' birthright (Gen. 27:18-36). Youthful Moses murdered an Egyptian (Exod. 2:11-12). Noah, that early boat-builder, apparently had an alcohol problem (Gen. 9:20-21). King David, one of the most revered religious personalities of the Old Testament, yielded to the temptation of immorality and even murder when he arranged to have Uriah killed in battle because he desired Uriah's wife, Bathsheba (2 Sam. 11).

Nor do we have to read the Bible for clergy sins. Religious "greats" have confessed to the frailty of their human natures. For example, the renowned architect of theology of the early church, Saint Augustine, confesses his struggles with immorality:

> The new will which I now began to have, by which I will worship you freely and to enjoy you, O God, the only certain joy, was not yet strong enough to overcome that earlier rooted deeply through the years. My two wills, one old, one new, one carnal, one spiritual, were in conflict and in their conflict wasted my soul.[1]

John Bunyan, who wrote the Christian allegory, *Pilgrim's Progress,* knew well the battle with evil. In a succeeding work, *Grace Abounding to the Chief of Sinners,* he confesses that:
—as a youth, he could "sin with the greatest delight and ease."
—he began to attend church services but found it "a full year before I could leave dancing."
—at times he vacillated between the peace of faith and the lure of temptation, and had the desire to "sell Christ."[2]

The apostle John expresses the matter succinctly when he says: "If we say we have no sin, we deceive ourselves, and the truth is not in us"(1 John 1;8).

No discussion of the spiritual battles in ministry would be complete without describing the sins which tempt some of the men and women who wear the robes of the church in our time.

Eight Sins of the Clergy

1. The greatest sin of the profession is to lose the passion for the Spirit, to become a cold ash instead of a living flame for God. This sin is the loss of the excitement of the spiritual quest. A good example is the pastor who is no longer challenged by the exciting question with which the Lord confronted Isiah, "Who will go for me?" (Isaiah 6:8)

I am speaking of the pastor who began ministry with a dedication to servanthood and discipleship, but who, over the years, loses that sense of devotion to the cause of Christ and finds the ministry is no longer a constant prayer but a boring burden. Such religious apathy is a sin because it brings death to the spirit.

2. Another sin of the clergy is exemplified by the pastors who feel that they should be, or appear to be, perfect. They fear being vulnerable in any way, must always be in control, and will not admit failure. Many pastors believe that they must be examples of faithful perfection—a fallacy which is encouraged by some parishioners, unfortunately.

The would-be-perfect-pastors insulate themselves from their people. Their facade keeps them from honestly sharing their weaknesses and strengths. Pastors who depend on themselves alone cannot fully relate to parishioners. There must be interaction with others for the spirit to grow.

The old cliche is helpful here: "Pastors are not called to be perfect, they are called to be faithful."

3. Another sin of the profession is to allow ourselves to be seduced by the materialistic culture in which we live, to be more influenced by wealthy social standards than challenged by the Christian values of life. Like the Hebrews who followed Aaron's worship of idols, forgetting the Ten Commandments, clergy can become infected with dependence upon possessions and things. (See Exod. 32:2-4.)

Too many pastors and church members measure their lives by cultural values instead of religious values to such an extent that many critics of the church say it has lost its prophetic voice by being captured by society.

Some of the decline in the influence of the church in our time may be caused by those pastors who measure their work largely in terms of size of salary, prestigious housing, and a number of additional benefits. Such overconcern for job security raises the interesting question, "How effective would Jesus have been if he made such demands a prior condition to his servanthood?"

4. Another sin is the act of succumbing to the temptation for power and prestige within the ecclesiastical structure of the church. An example is the pastor who fawns on the officials, fears to challenge the system when it is wrong, raises mission money for his record rather than for the need in the field, connives to move along into larger and more prosperous churches, and plays the game for his own advancement and influence. While aggressive tactics may be appreciated in business, self-advancement should not be the standard among clergy.

In spite of my peers who will disagree, when we consider a new parish, the questions should not be: "How much do they pay?" but rather, "What is the challenge?" and "Do I feel God wants me there?"

Our concern should not be "How nice is the parsonage?" or "How prosperous is the church?" but "Are the parish members willing to search for the riches of Christ with me and my family?"

5. The pastor who does not schedule appropriate time for study and development of growth in the Lord is in danger of falling into another kind of sin.

Preserving and strengthening the commitment to faith and practice is primary to the minister's charge. Almost every significant leader of the religious life, including John Wesley, Saint Francis, Mother Teresa, William Law, Thomas Merton, and others, followed a discipline of faith-growth. All of them pursued definite patterns of study and meditation, as well as practice.

It was unfortunate that, in turning away from so much of the Roman Catholic theology, Protestants also dismissed Roman Catholic disciplines of the spirit. We have much to learn from our brothers and sisters in Christ, not the least of which is their appreciation of the value of retreats, contemplation, and the use of spiritual guides.

Some pastors fail to attend continuing education courses because they cannot see their own professional inadequacies. Congregations should be more forceful in encouraging pastors to strengthen their ministerial weaknesses, whether as a preacher, an administrator, an educator, or worship planner.

6. Another sin for some clergy is to use professional code names such as "eschatology," "millenium," and "exegesis" to the detriment of the laypersons' understanding. We need to evaluate carefully the educational background and vocabulary of our congregation so that we speak within its limits. Too often our academic preparation leads us to employ terms that perplex rather than enlighten our constituents. Many pastors may preach eloquently, but if we leave the congregation wondering what we meant, we have sinned against the Holy Spirit by not being "a light to the Gentiles" (Acts 13:47).

("Eschatology" refers to that part of Christian doctrine which deals with the final end of man, the Second Coming of Christ, immortality, and the final judgment. "Millenium" refers to a suggested thousand year period in which the kingdom of God is to flourish (Rev. 20:2). "Exegesis" is an explanation or interpretation of the Bible.)

7. No list of sins would be complete if I did not mention the pastor's neglect of family. Many of us become seduced by the adulation of parish members whom we have served faithfully, instead of becoming seduced by the love of a faithful spouse and family. Too many of us tragically come to some point in life when we may have established ourselves well in our profession, but meet a fractured family when we go back to the parsonage. Many clergy divorces are based on this divergence of family goals. Sometimes congregations are to blame, perhaps unwittingly, for making exorbitant demands upon the pastor, which lead to family problems.

Ministers' children all too often find themselves neglected. "When are you going to be in your office? I need to talk with you about school." "When are you coming home?"

In our sinful pursuit of self-achievement we forget how critical parishioners can attack our spouses and children instead of confronting us. "Did you see her dress, well, I never" "Why don't they make their children behave?" "He only thinks of himself. Doesn't he love his wife." "Why should she work? We certainly pay him enough."

8. Sexual immorality and drug abuse must be added to this list. Both might well be claimed as occupational hazards of the professions, for both are escapes for overworked and stress-filled professionals of many types. But "escapes" they are, and they are more indicative of a loss of spiritual enthusiasm which often leads to immorality. Sexual deviation and drug abuse are not so much causes as results; they are sinful habits which come to fill lives made empty by the loss of spiritual disciplines.

There are a number of reasons why pastors, like other professional people, sometimes fall from grace and find themselves enmeshed in habits that undermine their work. It is not always the pressure of the job. It may be boredom: "There is not enough challenge in this church. It doesn't want to go anywhere." Dissatisfaction may be another reason: "I am not getting ahead fast enough." "My spouse cannot accept the demands that my job places on my family." There are even a few pastors who claim special privilege: "It's all right for me to slip once in a while. I'm a minister. I have a holy link with God."

Like a lot of other people, pastors have to pray without ceasing that we are filled with faith to withstand the fiery darts of the evil one.

In calling attention to the sins of the clergy I have not sought to be sensational. Rather, I have presented a side of the profession which is too often swept under the carpet by clergy themselves or dealt with in a holier-than-thou judgment by the public.

Clergy do intend to live special lives. In the ceremony of ordination we are called out of the world, we commit ourselves to be disciples of Jesus the Christ, and we are set apart to be ambassadors of our Lord in work and deed, in faith and spirit. It is to such a high calling that everyone of us dedicate our lives. Ordination does not exempt us from any of the moral standards of faith. In fact, we voluntarily place our lives in public view and knowingly stand before the world which watches our every move.

If clergy fall from their vision and their promises of discipleship, we are under the same obligation as every other man and woman—we are expected to confess and to ask forgiveness. We can make no excuse, we can claim no special privilege. If we disobey God we are obliged to ask God's mercy.

In a sense, we are not different from Everyman and Everywoman. All of us are children of God. All of us are caught in the "democracy of sin." All of us are called to confess our faults and seek reconciliation with our Creator. None of us has any more right to cast the first stone than those who gathered around the woman taken in adultery. Who of us has not fallen at times from the grace of God?

But there are those who will tell you they are not included in this group. Beware of the evangelist, author, or preacher who judges all of life, who casts stones of judgment and does not love enough to forgive.

Sins of the clergy? Of course, all of us learn through our mistakes, or as one pastor expressed it "We cannot love unless we have accepted forgiveness, and the deeper our experience of forgiveness is, the greater is our love" (Paul Tillich, in conversation).

. . . .

It is tempting in discussing the clergy's spiritual battles with "sin" to present the matter in general terms. It is so much easier to talk about "their sins" instead of facing the issues and admitting "my sins." Spiritual struggles are not general, they are personal.

I find a number of sins which burden my life as they may obstruct the lives of parishioners, too.

I need to be more conscientious about my relationship with God.

I do not spend enough time on prayer and meditation.

I struggle constantly with the material attractions of the world and the plain sincerity of the Christian life. I am more a captive of the things of our time than the spiritual powers of faith.

I am not courageous enough to challenge the powers of darkness such as political corruption, social injustice, and religious deceit.

On the other hand, I am a sacred, precious, valuable child of God.

I have been created by God and endowed with God's spirit of life.

I am accepted in spite of who I am. I have been bought with a price.

I am loved, comforted, empowered and directed by my Lord.

I am a part of the noblest cause of life; the visible and the invisible church.

I know the purpose and the plan for my life—to be a disciple of Jesus Christ, in thought, in word, and in deed.

But such solid faith does not make me complacent. My imperfect humanness has many ways of keeping me aware of my place—such as the time I was a coward.

"Spiritual Coward"

"You buried my mother two years ago, Pastor. You may have forgotten me, but I would like your help again."

He was right. I did not remember him or the occasion, but I agreed to officiate another time for the family.

When I went to the funeral home on the night before the service, I found only a few people there. I was surprised to observe that none of them seemed particularly upset.

"Can you make it as short as possible?" I was asked.

I agreed, and also interpreted the request to mean that they did not want me to spend any more time with the mourners.

The following day was an unusually busy one for me, so that I made up my comments on the way to the funeral home.

"No one seems to care," I said to myself. "I'll use an idea or two that I've used before, and I'll cut the service in half."

Only five persons showed up for the funeral, and I felt ridiculous standing behind the speaker's stand. It would have been far more meaningful, I thought, if the few of us had just gathered informally and shared our feelings.

Of the five, one man appeared completely oblivious to my presence, as he stared off into a corner of the room. An older couple seemed somewhat concerned but gave the impression they were just there to be polite. Only the brother of the deceased paid any attention as I read the scripture and added a few comments.

After the service, we drove to the cemetery in only two cars.

"This must be one of the largest funerals you have ever had," quipped the director.

It was cold at the cemetery, with the winter wind and light snow on the ground also suggesting, "Make it brief!" I did.

Afterward I went over to the brother, who was taking a rose from the casket.

"I hope you will find comfort that she is released from the cares of life," I said in a perfunctory manner. "I pray these moments were helpful to you."

"Yes," he replied. "I apologize for not talking with you at the funeral home last night. I was just too caught up in my emotions. You see, my sister was an invalid. In order to take care of her, I never married. So, for the past thirty years, I have been her life. I don't want to complain about it. The things I was able to do made her happy, and I feel it was what God called me to do. We could never go to church, though, because of her condition, but we listened to churches on the radio and used our TV. If it weren't for my faith, and hers, I don't know what I would have done. We really didn't have many friends. Somehow they just slipped away over the years. They didn't understand our predicament, I guess. As I say, my sister's ailment was not a pretty thing. She was deformed and crippled, but she sure had a beautiful heart. I know that. Yes, pastor, she was all the world to me except, that is, my Savior. I thank God that she's now in one of his many mansions. Praise the Lord."

I could hardly believe what I was hearing. I recalled how curtly I had read the scripture, and then cut short the service. I reflected on how I had listened to the unsympathetic advice of his children. In so doing, I had defrauded a religious man in probably the time of his greatest spiritual need. Instead of strongly supporting him in his beliefs, I had failed to faithfully testify to the meaning of God's love and God's message about resurrection. I had listened too much to the voices of an uncaring world and not enough to the inner voice of my own spiritual convictions.

Some persons might pass it off by saying, "Well, you win some and you lose some." Instead, I felt it was a time when I failed as a pastor and I determined not to do so again. Even though the world might not want to hear the word of the Lord, it was my job to preach it to the disbelievers, even as our Lord did.

. . . .

My spiritual cowardliness is symbolic of what troubles the church in our time. Too many of us clergy adjust to the world instead of being faithful to the gospel. We work hard, but our surroundings are so comfortable. We seem more concerned about ease and good salaries than servanthood. We are fearful of confronting the power structures about public evils. We lack the stern disciplines to be prophetic, and the faith-depth to be spiritual directors. Too many of us have been entrapped by the culture that our Lord calls us to reform.

When I review the pages of my journal, a useful method for recording religious insights as they come to us from time to time, I find an entry that expresses these feelings about the need for the pastor's life to be more faithful. It is titled, "The Old Lady."

"The Old Lady"

On the sidewalk today, I passed an old lady,
who appeared to be wandering aimlessly.
Her blank expression suggested "nobody at home";
much of her life had gone out of her being.
No one to see, no place to go, nothing to do.

I wanted to reach out to her,
to tell her that someone cared,
to take her for coffee, to show her some attention,
to listen to her memories of yesteryear,
to offer her some of my own,
and thus, for a moment,
renew the meaning of life for her.
But I did not. I let her go.

But she has not let me go! Her presence
charges me with the awareness of her kind:
the aged, the cast off, the forgotten, the frail,
shut away in stinking, wet-floored institutions,
ill-cared for by underpaid attendants;
crying, screaming, moaning, and quietly wasting away,
feebly appealing to be known and cared for and loved.
And I do nothing for her or them.

How easy to build fantasies of nobleness.
How difficult to really love the unlovely.
Lord, this sin stalks my heart,
Enable me to make my life more caring.

Ministry is not a profession of perfect clergy. Like the apostle Paul, "I do not do the good I want, but the evil I do not want is what I do" (Rom. 7:19) However, we are ambassadors of a loving and forgiving God, who does not measure us so much by what we do as what we try to do.

Like Paul, I see no point in dwelling on my shortcomings but rather confessing them and moving on to the work at hand: "forgetting those things which are behind and straining forward to what lies ahead I press on toward the goal . . ." (Phil. 3:13-14)

Pursing the God-like life is by no means easy. Every pilgrim reports long periods of doubt and dark nights of the soul. Seeking the will of God means overcoming our own self. Moving in that direction is a dramatic journey.

Lead Us Not Into Temptation

"Satan now is wiser than of yore,
And tempts by making rich,
not making poor."

—Alexander Pope, *Moral Essays, III,* ("Of the Use of Riches"),
1732

Dealing with Temptation

If any member of the clergy tells you that he or she has not
fought a spiritual battle with temptation, that person is a liar.
Every person is tempted, even as our Lord warned, "Temptations
to sin are sure to come"(Luke 17:1). A religious person is no
exception; even Paul struggled with temptations.

"I do not understand my own actions. For I do not do
what I want, but I do the very thing I hate . . . sin . . .
dwells within me. . . . I delight in the law of God, in my
inmost self, but I see in my members another law at war
with the law of my mind. . . . Wretched man that I am!
Who will deliver me from this body of death?" (Rom.
7:15-24)

Every person is tempted. Some of us are tempted by faithless friends. We may be tempted to cheat or be dishonest on our income tax or with our employers' goods. We may be tempted by ambition and power, as was our Lord when he was tempted to turn stones into bread. So many of us are tempted to put ourselves first. As our Lord said, there is no one without temptation.

An older former parishioner took great pleasure in quoting a poem which shaped his life and that has helped me with mine.

"There was an old soldier
    whom all must applaud.
He fought many battles
    both here and abroad.

But the greatest battle
    that he ever was in,
Was his battle with Self
    in the conquest of sin."[3]

In my struggles with temptation, I have a number of aids. First, there is my own conscience that tells me what I am doing is wrong. Unfortunately, it does not tell me strongly enough, and I continue giving in to what tempts me. But I do not fully enjoy it and actually find that my temptation is undermining my self-confidence. Like a submerged rubber ball, my guilt keeps bobbing to the surface of my life.

Scripture proves to be a help in my battle, especially the words by the disciple James who some authorities say was the Lord's brother.

"Count it all joy, my brethren, when you meet various trials, for you know that the testing of your faith produces steadfastness. And let steadfastness have its full effect, that you may be perfect and complete, lacking in nothing." (James 1:2-4)

I find that temptation tests me and develops my resolution to be strong. But I am always aware that the testing is no guarantee of victory! Perhaps it will be only by the grace of God that I will have the power to persevere towards release from my old self.

The example of Christian friends helps the most. It is not what they say so much as how they live that helps me. I respect them for their characters of faithfulness and I want them to respect me. I don't want to deceive them by my own weaknesses.

But it is not just their good conduct that impresses me, it is the knowledge that they are tempted, too. Their struggles give me courage. Their battles and their trials help me fight through my own.

Conscience, scripture, the example of friends, prayers, moral standards of others, and the grace of God—all these help us in times of temptation. But how?

In order to explain how conscience can direct us, how prayer helps and how God moves within us, my journal includes four real life spiritual struggles.

A. The Temptation of Other's Possessions
B. The Temptation of Doubt
C. The Temptation of The Affair
D. The Temptation of Drugs

Each spiritual battle is described in detail; even as the outcome appears to be uncertain.

A. The Temptation of Others' Possessions

Very early in my ministry a banker friend taught me how to deal with the temptation suggested by the tenth commandment, "Thou shalt not covet what is thy neighbor's."

A couple I knew were involved in a vicious divorce. One day the wife came to my office carrying a beautiful old-fashioned china lamp.

"Will you please keep this here at the church?" she implored. "If I leave it at home, my husband will smash it to bits."

Later she came to me with a large sum of money.

"I don't know what to do with this," she explained. "I'm afraid he will get it away from me, even if I put it in the bank."

The divorce later was granted, but by that time both the husband and wife were hospitalized and, not surprisingly. died. I found myself with someone else's possessions and no clear idea what to do with them. Fortunately, my banker friend advised,

"Put the money in a trust account for their small children. Someday they will grow up and need it."

It was a lesson in how to be a good steward, but little did I know how that experience would shape my future. Later, like many ministers, I would be asked to handle several large estates.

Clergy in the course of their calling meet widows, some of whom have been left considerable sums of money. It is not unusual for some widows to be attracted to a caring pastor, and sometimes that friendship results in the estate being left to the pastor, even though he or she may attempt to refuse such a gift. So it happened to me.

A widow who had no family left me her home and bank account because of the friendship we had developed when I, as her minister, had the opportunity to call on her often and help her on several occasions. I felt the gift was given more because I was a pastor than a friend. Morally then the assets belonged to the church, so I gave the funds, not in my name but in hers, to the congregation of which she had been a loyal member.

A second opportunity to be an honest and responsible steward in Christ's name occurred when an elderly man asked me about a large coin collection.

"When my wife passed away," he explained, "I had to go through her things. I was well aware that she was a collector of coins since her youth, but I had no idea about the extent of her collection. I found all sorts of coins hidden away among her things. I do not know their value. I'd appreciate it if you'd find out how much they're worth."

How easy it would have been to deceive the aged widower! But lessons concerning the pastoral role of steward support a minister at such times. I had the coins appraised and then with great pleasure informed my parishioner of a much larger return than he had expected from "just a few old coins."

Pastors are representatives of the church. Estates and other people's possessions come to us because we are clergy rather than because we are personally deserving. It would be a sin of covetousness to use the trust of any parishioner for our own gain.

B. Temptation of Spiritual Doubt

Becoming a minister demands idealism. It requires a willingness to see what the world might be instead of what it is. Those who would be Christians are called to live in two worlds, the world of hope and the world of reality. There have been numerous times when I, like many ministers, cry out, "How long, O Lord, how long is it going to take to change the evil of today into the promise of tomorrow?"

I feel surrounded by people who believe that human nature will not change. They do not live for a better world, they want to get theirs today. And, of course, they often do. I feel left at the gate, bypassed, like one who bet on the wrong horse. I doubt my faith, my self and my God.

My faith tells me that honesty is the best policy, yet I see friends who are dishonest with the government, deceitful with their wives or husbands, and cunning in their businesses. Still, they appear to prosper and seem to look on my profession of ministry as naive and simplistic. My faith tells me not to lay up treasures for myself but to be rich toward God. Yet I have friends of wealth and ease, and I wonder if being a low-paid pastor is worth it. I know people who have achieved business and political power. I wish I had such influence instead of having to admit that I live in an era in which church or ministry have very little acceptance.

Sometimes I doubt myself. I believe that I have been called to follow my Lord, and most of the time I do so gladly and with confidence. But there are periods when I feel weak and ineffective. My belief in my worth in the sight of God falters and I feel overwhelmed by my own failings. I see acquaintances, even clergy friends, who have such poise and social adeptness. They appear to have the world by the tail, while I am not sure of my role and feel humbleness to be a disgrace instead of a sign of grace.

And there are occasions when I doubt God, as I see evil persons succeeding in high places and selfish people enjoying the harvest of the land while the poor continue to suffer. I wonder, like so many others: "Doesn't God care?"

How many times I have cried out, "Is it worth it?" when the checkbook seemed low and the bills high; when others received promotions I thought my servanthood in the cause of Christ had earned; when my best sermons in God's name were greeted with coldness; or when some sacrificial act went unappreciated.

That reminds me of the doubts that assail me as I work with parishioners. They seem so hard to change. I wonder where God is with them. They appear so self-centered. Will they never be concerned about the gospel and the word? They look on the church as a social club. When will they come to worship God? They take so little interest in all my great suggestions, all my extraordinary sermons, and all my words of faith and wisdom.

Thus many kinds of doubts often confront me. Some of them I have learned to overcome, not because I have so much faith but because my job as pastor requires that once a week, at least, I deal with the Bible, the pulpit, and the hour of worship. Each of these draws me back to strength in the Lord. Each helps to revive my fainting soul.

But when I slip into serious times of faithlessness and deeper doubt, the solution is not so easy or immediate. It is far more complicated. The period of depression is longer, the time of recovery is lengthened, and the road back to faith is steeper. But through it all, I have learned that there are some traditional answers the church has offered down through the ages which are often helpful. All of us who are pastors resort to one or more of the disciplines of the faith to keep out spirits alive.

One of our first steps toward recovery of faith is to share our doubts with our peers in a professional support group to which many of us belong. These meetings are not unlike some prayer groups of laypersons. We meet voluntarily to form a close fellowship in which we share our fears, our pains, our doubts, and our achievements. We rely on each other for honest response and counsel. We support one another in times of adversity and rejoice among ourselves in times of victory. We grow in grace through prayer. We increase in faith through studying the word. In short, we share our concerns and thus discover that in fellowship our burdens become light.

Reading devotional books is another way to confront doubt and keep faith strong, but it should be noted at the outset that this kind of literature is not like any other. Some books record history, others tell stories, while additional volumes speak of science and art. On the contrary, devotional readings enlighten the soul. They do not speak about God; they are of God. They are not interested in academic discussion or debate but in revealing the Spirit. They are not written to express an opinion but to speak for a Presence, even as do the psalms which are the best example of devotionals. Like the Psalms, a devotional book is one which is read over and over again until its spirit becomes our spirit.

Prayer is of course another antidote to doubt, but prayer is easier to talk about than practice. When we are discouraged it is hard to pray. Even in good times we experience dry periods when our most sincere prayers appear to accomplish nothing. In either case, those experienced in prayer suggest that we just wait out the dry times, as one would wait for a storm to pass. They tell us the rejuvenation of prayer will always come. Another method of overcoming prayer-vacancy is to continue to read published prayers. If our own seem ineffectual, sometimes the prepared petitions of well-known religious leaders can express our needs for us and revitalize our spirits.

Writing a journal often helps to keep faith and spirit in good order. But journal-writing is not what it may seem. It is not a diary. It is not an autobiography. Nor is it a personal history of events. Rather it is a collection of observations and insights which break in upon a person from time to time and which are recorded as part of that individual's spiritual journey. For example, a journal could contain the content of dreams; feelings of particular anger, joy, or love; reflections upon a special emotional and spiritual experience; quotations which seem part of one's spiritual development; thoughts about the purpose and meaning of one's life; as well as pages in which the writer seeks to work out some inner problem of self and faith.

Not only does the writing of a journal bring freedom to the soul but rereading what has been written months or years ago provides new insights into a person's own character development or one's unfortunate lack of it.

If doubt has been one of the enemies of faith, the practice of making a retreat has been another traditional answer to that antagonist. Withdrawing from responsibilities for even a day, or what is better a week or even a month, is really not so much retreat as it is renewal. Pastors and laypersons retreat to go forward. We retreat in order to regain our strength and reaffirm our

104

vows, that we might serve more faithfully. We do not set aside these times to avoid the world. Instead, we spend time in silence, scripture reading, reflection, prayer, journal writing, recreation, and rest—all to the end that we may return to the needs of the world with greater strength and deeper commitment in the name of Christ.

As with every human being, doubt about ourselves, our role in life, and even about God afflicts us all. It always has. But the church supports its own, and with such disciplines as we have mentioned saves those who would perish and inspires those who might fall. If we doubt, our Lord reaches across the water of life to hold us up as he did for Peter(Matt. 14:31). Or, if we continue to doubt as did Thomas, Jesus appears to us in many different ways to assure us of his presence.

C. Temptation of the Affair

"The most intimate thing I see about my husband is his dirty underwear," she told me. "I miss my sex life desperately!"

I was visiting a couple I had married many years before. I had learned that their marriage was in difficulty and went to see if they wanted help. Unfortunately, soon after I arrived the husband had to answer a service call, so I spent an hour talking with the wife, hoping that he would return. At first, her conversation dealt with their family problems, but as time passed, she talked more about her feelings toward me.

"I could not have an affair with just anyone," she suggested, "but sometimes I think I could be tempted by someone I really trusted."

Then she added, with a twinkle in her eye, "You could be that person."

Of course, therapists, counselors, and doctors may evoke such responses of attachment, but pastors are certainly not immune.

Clergy are trained to be lovers. They are called to "love others" as they have been loved by Christ. They are charged to love a congregation. They learn how to care for people, giving them sympathy, attention, and support. They sometimes share their own problems as a method of helping troubled church members understand themselves. Furthermore, clergy are available, friendly, and trained to show interest. So parishioners may develop fantasies about them. But it is not just a one-way street. There are occasions when pastors will violate the role of professional counselor and take advantage of those who seek their help.

Rev. Mr. Smith was a young, energetic pastor of a suburban church. He was active in the community and served on many committees. Although he appeared to be well accepted by his peers, there were indications that he did not understand himself. On several occasions, he allowed his own unsolved needs to violate the trust of a counseling situation.

"He told me I was a very sexy woman, and that he would like to see more of me," one of his parish members reported, as she explained to her friends why she was dropping out of Smith's Bible class.

. . . .

Mrs. Jones was having troubles with her husband because of his excessive gambling. She went to her pastor for advice. For him, her visit was an interesting hour in the middle of a dull day. He suggested another session. He found her exciting, and he was pleased when she listened as he began to tell her of his own frustrations. So they shared more and more. She knew he could not reveal confidences, and he discovered that she was willing to develop their relationship further. They continued to meet, using the excuse of church business, and then, when that reason wore thin, to see each other out of town.

But their affair was always touched with fear. He remembered an incident in which an irate husband had stood up in church on a Sunday morning and called the preacher out of the pulpit because of his infidelity. She feared that their secret lives might be discovered by their spouses, with the possibility of ensuing violence. The specters of a church scandal, ouster of the minister, divorce in their families, or the loss of valued friends were always with them.

. . . .

From time to time we hear of the doctor or clergyman who is charged with illicit relationships with a patient or church member.

"How could Dr. Brown or Rev. Green do such a thing?" the public asks.

I know how. I've been there.

One day I called at the home of a married woman to inquire about her chronically ill father. They both appreciated my visit, so I called again and then again. However, every time I visited, I came away with a growing anxiety about my real motives: ministry to a sick man or personal interest in an attractive woman?

Although I was married, I found myself searching for excuses to return to the home. But at the same time I was praying for strength that would enable me to find peace by staying away.

Sometimes I mused: "What are you being such a Puritan about? Other people think nothing of having an affair. They do it all the time. They claim it is important to have such experiences in order to know more about living. Am I going to shrivel up in frustrated desire, or am I going to fulfill my being?"

I thought of the advice of the Book of Proverbs:

> My son, keep my words . . .
> to preserve you from the loose woman. . . .
> I have perceived among the youths . . .
> a young man without sense,
> passing along the street near her corner . . .
> in the twilight, in the evening,
> and, lo, a woman meets him. . . .
> She seizes him and kisses him . . .
> "I have decked my couch with coverings. . . .
> I have perfumed my bed with myrrh. . . .
> Let us take our fill of love till morning.
> Let us delight ourselves with love!" . . .
> He follows her as an ox goes to the slaughter. . . .
> He does not know that it will cost him his life.
> —(Prov. 7:1-23)

That passage was a strong restraint on my own emotions, but I rationalized to avoid its judgment.

"Perhaps it does not apply to me," I said. "After all I am not a youth, and the person who could give me peace is not a designing woman out of Proverbs but a respected neighbor. Proverbs are only words. They're cold and unfeeling. How can they understand my desire or the emptiness of my heart?"

I even said to myself, "Maybe I could make up for the sin of my body by more prayers of my soul. Aren't we taught that there is forgiveness with God?"

Often, as I struggled with my feelings, I identified my situation with other examples from the Bible. I recalled how King David, that heroic religious leader of the Israelites, seduced the beautiful wife of Uriah. I observed that people of faith, even deep faith, can be caught up in the enticement of immorality.

On the other hand, I thought of Joseph, the young man who was sold by his brothers. I remembered how he was enticed by the wife of Pharaoh and how he overcame that temptation. It helped to believe that faith could "deliver us from evil."

The more I saw of my parishioner, the more my inner battle continued to rage. I felt my soul was an arena in which wild combatants struggled for my very life itself. Desire contended with virtue; "Eros" grappled with "Agape" and "The Devil" fought with "God."

Nor was my battle quickly decided. It continued for months. Some of my visits were filled with desire, others with virtue; some with Eros others with Agape.

However, as I continued to call, a number of questions tormented me. What was missing in my life that I thought the woman could fulfill? What kind of a relationship did I really want? What did her qualities of life have to do with my interest in her? What would the whole thing mean to my own marriage? Might the situation cause me to give up the ministry?

So I continued to reflect and to pray, but I soon realized that neither effort was solving my condition. I needed the help of someone more experienced than I, who could give me some more direct guidance than my undeveloped understanding of myself and God. That was why I went to a counselor. Talking my problem through took many sessions. Many of them were painful, but I began to know my own self better, to confront some of my inner conflicts, and to find how I was going to overcome the struggle I was in.

Faith also helped. Prayer reminded me that I was created by God. As a child of God, I had the freedom to do what I wanted. But I could expect to face the consequences, even as the prodigal son (Luke 15:11-32).

Furthermore, prayer reminded me that I had marriage vows to respect, the heritage of a family name to be proud of, and the professional standing of minister to protect for my own future, as well as the reputation of ministry for my colleagues.

I also became more aware of my obligation to the woman herself. If my motives were anything less than honest, our friendship might turn sour. The fair weather of the moment might, when it began to involve our spouses, become a dangerous storm of tomorrow.

After all this, when I continued to see her it was on a different basis, in the spirit of a different person. Our relationship was changed. We discovered new interests, all of which could withstand the inspection of friends, as well as the judgment of our consciences.

What might have been an exciting but immoral and sinful affair, such a common theme in literature and films, became for me a relationship that deepened in trust and caring instead of a situation ending in brokenness or violence. I had been saved from the destructive consequences of immorality by a good therapist, the power of prayer, the forgiveness of God, and the guidance of the Holy Spirit.

D. The Temptation of Drugs

I was becoming more and more frustrated with my job as a minister. I felt people did not really want to grapple with questions about their faith. My counseling load seemed to get heavier and longer. So I found myself relying on the afternoon pick-up or a couple of drinks after supper. This pattern seemed to work pretty well until one day I was forced to see myself in a new light.

I had gone to a local liquor store to restock my supply. As I entered, a customer collapsed on the floor right in front of me. In his hand he clutched a paper bag obviously containing a bottle.

The liquor salesman came from behind the counter and together we helped the man to his feet, encouraging him to brace himself against a stack of beer cases.

"Are you driving?" the clerk asked me, hoping for some way to get the man out of the place.

"Yes, my car's out front," I answered.

"He will never be able to make it home by himself. Would you give him a lift?"

I replied that I would, asked for a bottle of Scotch, paid my bill, and turned my attention to the unsteady drinker. I half-supported the man to my car, he gave me his address somewhat incoherently, and I drove the man to his home.

He lived in an expensive area, and I was anxious about how he would be received when I got him to the door.

At first, no one answered when I rang the bell. When I looked through the glass-paneled door, I saw two children playing on the floor near a lighted Christmas tree. I wondered what they would think when their father staggered into the house.

After several monents, a tall, blonde, neatly-dressed woman came. She took charge of the situation immediately.

"Where did you find him?" she asked. Her manner suggested that he had arrived in a similar condition previously, and she needed to know where to get his car keys or other personal belongings.

I described the liquor store, and as I helped her get him through the doorway, she added, "The clinic warned me this would happen. I thought I could handle it. God help us, if we don't go the hospital now."

I turned to go, but was curious about the effect of the situation on the children. I looked at the boy. He gave me a "so-he's-done-it-again" shrug. The younger girl had disappeared, and as I tried to see if she was in the nearby dining room, a loud noise diverted my attention. The man had fallen over a chair and was sprawled out behind the sofa.

The situation suddenly seemed out of control and increasingly embarrassing, so I quickly said good-bye and walked out into the crunching snow with my mind in a turmoil.

110

I could not help comparing myself with the man I had just brought home. Like him, I had gone to the liquor store. Was that the way he started on the road to apparent alcoholism? Was I now on the way to such a problem? Why was I the one who happened by and was asked to take the man home? Why did I meet his despairing wife and see his disgusted children?

My questions forced me to conclude that I was in the presence of evil. It was a tremendous experience. I saw judgment upon myself, but that was not all. I learned something terribly significant about evil: Evil has a weakness which opens it to its own death! We can learn from evil. It can be an illustration of what should be. It can point the way to God. I had discovered the Achilles heel of evil. I had found its mortal weakness. Evil illuminates the Good. It points the way to its own destruction. Evil revealed me to myself in that incident of sinfulness. It directed me toward my own salvation.

I thanked God for the evil I had seen.

But the demon of Evil is not without a quiver full of arrows. The desire to drink is not easily overcome, if conquered even for a time. The "pleasures" of yesteryear are still remembered when the accompanying pain has been forgotten. Constant vigilance is a habit alcoholics cultivate. And part of that habit, at least for me, is the importance of reminding myself over and over of the deceit in the bottle.

> Do not look at wine when it is red,
>> when it sparkles in the cup
>> and goes down smoothly.
> At the last it bites like a serpent,
>> and stings like an adder. (Prov. 23:31-32)

I have been a victim of this serpent too long not to know it fakes death and lies in wait until it can strike again. But I have found the power to slay the demon, whenever he raises his head, through my reliance upon my faith in Jesus Christ, who makes all things new, even me.

But Deliver
Us from Evil

"All spirits are enslaved
which serve things evil."

—Shelley, *Prometheus Unbound*, Act II, sc. 4

Civil Laws vs. Moral Laws

To be able and willing to read extensively concerning all types
of subjects is one of the requirements for good preaching and
ministry. Following such a discipline, I was rereading American
history, when I came to a phrase that has had a great effect upon
my life ever since.

"Your beliefs in God are heresy to our ears," it said. "You shall
be whipped and cast out from us!"

These were not the words of some pagan persecutor, but of
Christian church leaders in the Massachusetts Bay Colony in the
seventeenth century.

I read on to discover that the early settlement was controlled
by clergymen who used their clerical power to force all the colo-
nists to worship according to strict rules of conformity. Most
people obeyed, but a few did not.

Among those who refused was Mary Dyer. Mary was a Quaker and a very courageous one at that. She protested strenuously against the denial of religious freedom. She said all people should have the right to worship as they pleased.

For her pains, Mary Dyer was banished to the neighboring colony of Rhode Island. She did not stay there but soon returned to campaign for religious liberty again. She was arrested and in September, 1659, was sentenced to hang, along with two convicts.

The men were hung for their crimes, but at the last moment Mary was reprieved, probably because she was a woman. Her narrow escape did not stop her. Indeed, her courage and religious conviction about freedom of worship could not be silenced, and she was arrested and condemned a second time.

On June 1st, 1660, at Boston Common, Mary Dyer stepped up to the gallows with the prayer: "For those who do it in the simplicity of their hearts, I do desire the Lord forgive them."

Later as her body swayed and turned, one of the bystanders observed: "Mary Dyer did hang as a flag for others to take example by!"

Was the statement a warning to the faint-hearted to save their lives? Or was it a call to persons of conscience to defend the laws of God against the imperfect laws of man?

. . . .

Laws must be made for the order of society. As a matter of fact, the Bible teaches that God orders human life through the power of governing authorities.

> Let every person be subject to the governing authorities. For there is no authority except from God, and those that exist have been instituted by God. Therefore, he who resists the authorities, resists what God has appointed. (Rom. 13:1-2)

Even the apostle Paul in the New Testament urges that Christians must uphold the laws, or there will be chaos.

But laws made with even the best of intentions may prove to be unjust and not in the common good. They may meet civic standards but not more fundamental moral principles. They may

113

serve the state but not the Lord. Thus human laws need to be examined.

For example, the Old Testament includes the story of Daniel, that prophet of conscience, who refused to obey a law, even one made by "Presidents and princes" of Babylon, that declared that the only type of worship that would be allowed was the worship of King Darius. When Daniel continued to pray to the God of his own Hebrew people and not to the Babylonian king, he was cast into a den of lions. Miraculously he survived the punishment. His example of courageous conscience so impressed King Darius that he reexamined the repressive law, withdraw it, and permitted the Hebrew strangers to have their religious freedom. (See Daniel 6)

In the New Testament, our Lord dealt with this same problem in the phrase, "Render to Caesar the things that are Caesar's, and to God the things that are God's." The laws of the state must be respected, but when they infringe upon the moral codes they must be challenged. Many times our Lord confronted the authorities in this respect.

A sermon that appears political in content may in fact be the work of a prophetic pastor reminding us that we need to hew closer to the will of God than to the laws of the state. Every religious leader has been faced with this choice, for we dwell in the world but our citizenship is in heaven!

This loyalty to the will of God was ably illustrated by the prophet Amos, the shepherd of Tekoa who preached in the times of Uzziah the King of Israel. Amos condemned his own country for its worldly transgressions. "I hate your ceremonies of state," he said, "it would be more important to espouse justice and righteousness" (Amos 5:21,24, paraphrased). In just such a spirit, the clergy of today must address the condition of America in our time.

Whether the issues before us be the poverty of the Third World, the hunger of a part of all nations, the denial of human rights, the threat of nuclear anniliation, or the spectre of violence—all these call us to examine our principles and policies in the light of the word of God.

"Thus Says the Lord"

For the seven transgressions of America
    I will not revoke punishment:

    1. For your former dreams of faith and freedom,
        you have substituted
        ambition for wealth and power;

    2. Your American lifestyle seeks
        comforts instead of causes,
        sensuality in place of the Spirit,
        things before thinking;

    3. You put your individual selves
        before the Blessed Community;

    4. You consume more than your share
        of the world's goods and food,
        while starvation and poverty
        plague a third of all my people;

    5. You profiteer on the fears of your neighbors
        and have become a broker of war;

    6. Violence, the offspring of inequality and prejudice,
        stalks your streets,
        yet you will not listen to Me;

    7. You are prepared to maim and burn and kill
        millions of my children
        with nuclear bombs
        you call defense;

I supplied you with vision and resources,
    to become the leader among nations;
    but immorality and selfishness
    have weakened your resolve and your faithfulness.

Your sins can make you blind and will cause your power
　　　to stumble.
I am a God of judgment. I can raise up peoples
　　　to discipline you. You can be humbled by those
　　　whom you have exploited.

But if you return to Me, I will repent of My judgment.

For I am a God of love. I can bless your land
　　　with harvests, and I can bring your people to Peace.

Possessions or Spirit

Clergy in our time are not only confronted with the choice
between Caesar and God, but we are caught in the same dilemma
which threatened the early Hebrews. We want our idols instead of
the commandments.

We worship things instead of theology. We invest in the power
of possessions instead of the power of faith. We rely upon the
amount of our income instead of the amount of our beliefs.

Oftentimes we judge each other's progress in ministry by the
size of one's church. Numbers of membership impress us more
than another pastor's commitment to the gospel. We think in
terms of getting a bigger parish than living a more dedicated life.
We adopt worldly criteria for "success."

Not only are many of us confronted with the spiritual battle
of servanthood, but we are confronted by many within our own
ranks who believe that self-denial in the name of Christ is out of
date. They refer to places in scripture where God promises
prosperity in return for righteousness: "Be careful to do the words
of this covenant, that you may prosper in all that you do" (Deut.
29:9). There are clergy who preach a gospel of comfort and financial affluence as the God-promised rewards of faithfulness.

Comfort, ease, and a full stomach insulate us from the cries of
the hungry, a sizeable bank balance protects us from feeling the

116

passion of poverty, and praying in a comfortable office dulls us to
the urgency of injustice. It is not surprising that the prophet John
the Baptist wore a hair-shirt or that Jesus lived a plain and simple
life.

"The Tombstone of America"

1981

A warm summer day, town of Manchester,
corner of Grove and Spring,
on the edge of the. village.

A young hitchhiker,
stands close by the highway,
with thumb up for a ride.

I drive by
in my old beat-up sedan,
veteran of thousands of miles,
and a multitude of repairs.

"Get in, friend," I say.
(I have nothing to lose.)

> For the next ten miles,
> we share our experiences
> and become brothers of the same land.

1984

A warm summer day, town of Manchester,
corner of Grove and Spring,
on the edge of the village.

A young hitchhiker,
stands close by the highway,
with thumb up for a ride.

I drive by
in my new imported and expensive car,
electric windows, tinted glass,
reclining seats, built-in stereo.

"Sorry," I murmur to myself.
(I have so much to lose.)

> For the next ten miles,
> I am alone and silent,
> aware of my fears and anxiety,
> lonely in my own land.

"1981—1984"

Numerals on a tombstone marked "America,"
in the cemetery of nations.

At the service attended by millions,
a lone preacher reads:
"Thou shalt not make unto thyself any graven image!"

So many people went away, wondering what the words meant.

For Thine
Is the Power

"Provided that God be glorified,
we must not care by whom."

—St. Francis de Sales, *Spiritual Conference 8*

Powers of the Spirit

Two of the most significant men of the Bible, the prophet
Isaiah in the Old Testament and Jesus in the New, attribute the
energy, purpose and inspiration of their lives to the Spirit. Each
declared:

> The spirit of the Lord is upon me,
> because the Lord has anointed me
> to bring good tidings to the afflicted;
> he has sent me to bind up the brokenhearted,
> to proclaim liberty to the captives,
> and the opening of the prison to those
> who are bound,
> to proclaim the year of the Lord's favor. . . .
>
> (Isa. 61:1; cf. Luke 4:18)

119

These words of Isaiah and our Lord constitute the marching orders for the minister. They define very strongly the purpose and mission of all we do. They are basic to the meaning of ministry and the direction of our work. If the Spirit is central to the life of Isaiah and to Jesus, it must be the core of the role of the pastor.

Not one of us can do anything for God or Christ unless the Spirit is upon us. That power, so often prayed for through the Lord's Prayer, is primary to all that we do. Our mission is dependent upon and begins with the Spirit. Before either Isaiah or Jesus began their ministries, they claimed the Spirit was upon them.

It is the power of the Spirit that moves us to help the afflicted. It is the energy of the Spirit that enables us to succor the downhearted. It is the courage provided by the Spirit that helps us to release the captives and prisoners of life's unjust circumstances. It is the passion of the Spirit that moves us to proclaim the time of the Lord is at hand.

No discussion of the various responsibilities of the pastor, such as we have seen in the previous pages, would be complete without a clear reference to the source of the pastor's power, that is the Spirit. Nor could we conclude this book on the work of the pastor without particular concern with that which in every pastor's soul is called the spiritual life.

Therefore, these last chapters of *Only By Grace* turn away from the clergyperson's daily professional decisions and concentrate instead on the pastor's spiritual life: what it is, how to define it, and how it manifests itself.

We are now living in a time when there is much emphasis upon the Spirit and the spiritual life. Voices claiming to speak for the Spirit are springing up everywhere. Many may be authentic but, because of the proliferation of "authorities," there may be the danger that we are hearing some false prophets.

It is in such times that we need to have some criteria for evaluating the presence of the Spirit and the spiritual life. Of course, neither can be circumscribed, but there are some reliable indications of the presence of each.

The well-known English author of the spiritual life Evelyn Underhill offers us just such an evaluation. She suggests there are three indices of spiritual development.

1. "There is a *profound sense of Security,* of being safely held in a cosmos of which, despite all contrary appearances, peace is the very heart.

2. "The relationship is felt rather as the intimate and reciprocal *communion of a person with a Person . . .* for it is always in a personal and emotional relationship that man finds himself impelled to surrender to God.

3. "Spirit is felt as *an overflowing power,* a veritable accession of vitality; energizing the self, or the religious group, impelling it to the fullest and most zealous living." (italics added)

To author Underhill's list, I would like to add a fourth which has been suggested by other teachers and prophets.

4. The Spirit has the capacity to intervene in a person's life, to heal suffering, to redirect purposes and emotions toward the will of God.

It would defeat the purpose of this explanation of the Spirit if I left these four indices of spiritual development in such an academic type of listing. In such a state they appear as dry bones. In order to bring the criteria to life with actual illustrations, I reach into my own experiences.

Powers of the Spirit: Security

1. *The spiritual life brings us a profound sense of security, of being safely held in the cosmos, despite all contrary appearances.*

One of the occupational hazards of clergy is to become involved in a power struggle with a faithful parishioner. Pastors are trained to lead. They feel they are ambassadors of God to the life of the parish. On the other hand, loyal members are duly elected by the membership to govern, and they want to exercise their power too.

So each vies for control. Each believes he or she should make the crucial decisions for the church.

It was in just such a common confrontation that I once found myself. Little did I know when it began that the conflict would reveal the power of the Spirit.

Security—"Thank You, My Enemy"

"You're a liar!" he shouted from across the room, "and what's more, you're a phony!"

We were at it again. I as the minister and he as an important member of the parish. We had been bitter enemies for months.

The problem was that each of us wanted to manage the church. He claimed that, as president of the congregation, he should make all of the decisions. I was concerned that everyone have a vote. He charged that my way was too slow, and nothing ever got done. I concluded that he wanted to be a dictator.

Every time an issue came up, we would be on opposite sides. Our earlier discussions became arguments. Our mutual distrust increased. Indeed, it seemed as though our differences had a ripple effect on all other matters. Every church meeting became charged with our emotions and complicated by our differences.

I found myself hating everything the man did. I suspected every move he made.

"He must be sick," I said to myself. "He isn't fair, he's under-handed and deceitful."

I would be naive not to conclude that he had similar feelings toward me.

Then one evening, when we argued more than usual, an older woman of the congregation asked if she might say a few words. Inasmuch as she rarely spoke, everyone listened intently.

"You two men," she began in a high-pitched voice while pointing directly at us, "make me sick. You act like spoiled children. Can't you be more Christian?"

As she spoke, I noticed many people nodding their heads in agreement.

That was all she said. Complete silence followed. Out of embarrassment, I think, the chairman adjourned the meeting.

122

I disliked her criticism. I felt put down, but I knew she was right. Nor could I get her remark out of my mind. I felt it was up to me to do something.

"After all, I'm a part of the church," I reflected. "I'm expected to be able to handle controversy, as well as myself. Difference of opinion is one thing, emotional hatred is another, and my faith doesn't allow for that."

The more I thought about it, the more I resolved to change in some way. So when I met the man again, I said:

"I don't feel we are listening to each other. Tell me again what you think we ought to do."

"You know damn well what I think," he snorted, "and I don't trust you anyhow. You're a phony, I tell you."

The weeks passed. I continued to hang on. "Give him time," I said to myself, "He will cool down."

It was, however, a false hope. Instead of defusing his anger, I found it was becoming more intense. Apparently, he was interpreting my efforts at understanding as weakness. So I kept wondering, "How can I break the pattern of anger exciting anger, hatred calling forth hatred?" I considered giving in to his demands and letting him try things his way, but I decided against that because I did believe in my point of view and I feared I might let others down who believed in it, too.

My parishioner was an honorable and honest man, hardworking and industrious, but I could not understand why he became so emotional. Was it related to some personal matter? Did he have money problems? What was going on at his job? How was his health? Whatever the cause, I concluded I really could not have much influence upon it. If there was to be any change, any solution to our relationship, it was going to be up to me. The only part I could change was myself.

But how to "change myself?" I spent much time just thinking about the question, often during long periods of silence that seemed to allow me to think more clearly, both about myself as well as my "enemy." My meditation helped me see his good qualities: his many years of loyalty to the church, the hours he had spent in special repair jobs, and his business skill as a trustee.

My silence and reflection also revealed to me a new appreciation of my own personhood. I experienced a development of my inner security, and the increased serenity brought with it a feeling of personal power. I felt I could accept his disagreements with more tolerance and meet his anger with more understanding and self-control.

All this moved me to the point where I began to feel very differently toward the whole matter. When we met again, I was able to be self-assured and in command of myself, even in the face of his continued and exaggerated hostility.

My new found positiveness was a joy to experience. It freed me from becoming entangled in his emotional net, and as the weeks passed, I found each confrontation a further test of my new self-control. I even began to look forward to the meetings as times to test my development.

Now those years of disturbing controversy are long past. I never did convince that man or change his constant attacks. Nevertheless, I am quite indebted to him, for through that experience I personally found the power to accept anger and to meet hatred with peace. I want to thank him because he moved me to acknowledge the anger in my own soul, deal with it, overcome it, and finally discover the reality of the lines:

"Thou preparest a table before me in the presence of my enemies"(Psalm 23:5).

Reflection upon this experience convinces me that there was something else at work on my soul than just my own anger and accompanying frustration. Something slowly took hold of my emotions, which were out of my control, and gave me instead an inner peace. I was given a profound sense of security in contrast to the feelings of hatred which had been destroying me as well as my parishioner.

I experienced one of the criteria for a spiritual experience, I found an inner peace in the face of all contrary appearances.

Powers of the Spirit: A Person

2. There is an indication that the spirit is present when we experience a sublime feeling of being in communication with a Person.

A Person—"Somebody Spoke"

Early in my ministry, like many young men, I had a number of youthful desires which tugged at my heart but which were not acceptable in proper company. I guess I was like Augustine, that early leader of the church, who enjoyed youthful habits and yet knew he would have to give them up in his search for maturity.

I sought the counsel of an older pastor but, unfortunately, his advice or my inability to hear left me with even more anxiety. Then an unexpected event occurred at a summer conference for clergy I attended.

Part of our study was to conduct worship for small churches in the area. One day a friend asked me if I would assist him by reading the scripture. I agreed.

When we arrived at the church it proved to be a log chapel in the woods, which was attended by summer vacationers. I took my place in the chancel and waited for my turn to read the day's lesson. Then it happened! I read the words, but as I did I had a strange feeling that they were directed, not toward the small congregation, but were spoken by some unknown Power specially to me! I felt uncomfortably warm, even though it was not a hot day. I can even recall wiping my brow. Then I was almost overcome with an inner peace and a feeling of great tranquility. I sat down after the reading, scarcely realizing that people sat in front of me in the pews. I had been far away. I felt I had actually been touched by something greater than myself, but I did not understand what.

As I have reflected upon that strange incident, I am still awed by it. The words which I had read were from Isaiah, "Though your sins be as scarlet they shall be as white as snow" (Isa. 1:18). I admit that I had gone to that chapel deeply conscious of my anxiety over my personal immorality. I was aware that guilt was burdening my life and I knew that some change was necessary, but I did not know how to bring it about. Obviously the words spoke to my condition. But why with such force? Why did I feel they were spoken by someone directly to me? Why did I experience the forgiveness which the words suggested? Why did I believe the scripture when several counseling sessions with my pastor-friend had not previously helped?

There are those who will suggest that it can all be explained psychologically. That may have been the case except for one factor. I felt I was spoken to by Someone who knew me. I felt I was forgiven by a Power that could really forgive me. I had the feeling something or Someone knew me so well it could break into my life.

Powers of the Spirit: Vitality

3. *"Spirit is felt as an overflowing power, a veritable accession of vitality, energizing the Self or religious group, impelling it to the fullest and most zealous living."*

Pastors are familiar with this definition. They recognize the connection between Spirit and vitality. When they feel the Spirit, they experience new power, extra joy in their work and a renewed zest for the Christian cause. They are usually among the first to claim:

"It is not I but the Spirit which lives within me. I am not myself, it's the Spirit which gives me energy. With the Spirit I am more than I am."

Persuasive evangelists seem touched with this energy of the Spirit as they preach to thousands. TV preachers appear to have extraordinary zeal to cure the afflicted as well as plead for money. Popular speakers about the power of faith tour the land testifying with unusual vitality about the Lord. And personable clergy energize individual congregations into phenomenal growth.

When we experience these popular religious leaders, how do we differentiate between planned, dramatic activity and the still small voice of spiritual vitality?

Damaged Church and Damaged Souls

I served a church of fourteen hundred members. It was a dedicated congregation which created and carried out a multitude of programs and projects. I, too, enjoyed the many opportunities to learn and to share, but after a number of years I began to wonder what I was doing. I was encouraging religious activity, but was I really helping to develop spiritual vitality? We were active but were we really changing lives? How deeply was our busyness penetrating human souls?

I am not criticizing the congregation. I am saying that I became troubled about my own spiritual growth. I was involved in many things, but was my life being changed by Christ? I had learned the religious language of the middle class but I found it no longer filled my spirit.

This concern disturbed me until, after meditation and prayer, I knew I had to make a change. I felt my relative ease in a well-to-do parish needed to be challenged. Would I be as confident about my faith if I faced the constant crises of threatening evils such as are found in the worst part of a city: destitution, utter despair, violence of all kinds, and hopelessness. I wanted to experience these situations to test my understanding of life and the power of the gospel. So I talked over my spiritual quest with my denominational superiors.

"There is an old congregation which is struggling to stay alive," they told me. "Once it was affluent but it has fallen upon hard times. The area is rough and the situation very difficult. Racial antagonisms and the presence of gangs infect the neighborhood. The members are faithful, but their resources of hope and money are about gone!"

It was just what I was looking for.

So I resigned from a specially fine suburban congregation and moved to three threadbare living rooms in an old church set amidst pot-holed streets in a deteriorating section of the city.

The new location was in even more difficult straights than my advisors had suggested. A few industrious projects had been undertaken in the past to upgrade the property, but by the time I arrived most members had concluded that the days of the parish were numbered, so they were doing nothing. One or two programs for the children of the neighborhood had been attempted, but they were often broken up by delinquent older gang members.

The church was dying. It was quite inactive, but in the midst of that inactivity many of us found the spiritual vitality about which Evelyn Underhill was speaking. The fewer we became as a congregation, the more important and open we became with each other. Feelings and beliefs which had been hidden for years came to the surface, as we found a new depth to our fellowship in Christ. When the organist left along with the choir, all of us had to sing louder. If there were to be any music, any praying, any testimonies, it was up to each of us to provide it. Our worship became more personal and more vital. When the church temporarily ran out of money, I served without pay, and this had the effect of drawing pew and pulpit much closer together.

As the final arrangements for closing came nearer, emotions ran high but even then our differences were touched with such concern for the church that we became more real to one another. It seemed that in death we were finding a new vitality about our faith.

Finally the inevitable happened: the building was sold, the church disbanded, and the remaining members dispersed to neighboring congregations. But for me, those few years were not an end but a new appreciation for faith and life. The three threadbare rooms had become a cathedral of prayer, as the difficulty of that situation forced me to my knees time after time to find courage and hope. The members taught me a new understanding of love through friendship with such parishioners as an eighty-year-old former school teacher, an Italian bird-man, a hard-driving union steward, a parish leader with classic character, a conscientious church historian, and two sisters who faithfully combined music and world travel.

In summary, I left a thriving, active parish at a time when I personally had lost my religious enthusiasm and vitality. I moved to a dying, inactive church where, in serving people in desperate need, I regained my trust in God and found my own spiritual renewal.

Another illustration of the power and energy of spiritual vitality, in a place one would least expect to find it, is the congregation of Rev. Joe Brown. He serves a church few other pastors would want. It is an area of economic blight. Most if not all of the parishioners subsist on welfare. An attitude of low self-esteem pervades almost everyone. They feel society has rejected them, and to a large extent, it has. Most of the residents and tenants are handicapped, not all can read or write, many of the women have been sexually abused, and most of the men cannot get any kind of jobs because of their lack of education and skills. A number of the youth have alcoholics and drug abusers for parent role models. Psychologists might describe many of the people as damaged, physically, emotionally, and spiritually.

In the face of such a parish, I asked Joe Brown what kept his own spirit alive and vital.

"The cross and resurrection of our Lord are absolutely essential to my faith," he explained. "If I did not believe that in my gut, I could not serve here. These people carry all sorts of crosses, but when I can help them accept their conditions and share their pain and suffering with others in the church, then I see resurrection beginning. Of course, only a few will fully recover. They're too enmeshed in their own problems for that. But I've supported many of them as they found forgiveness, and I've seen many find new lives for themselves by the grace of God."

As he spoke, I was reminded of the women who had begun a new life in the caring fellowship of the church. She marked her change of lifestyle by taking the only job available to her at the time, a position as night attendant in a shelter for homeless men. Soon after she began, she discovered that many of the men, either because of alcoholism or age, urinated in their own clothes while they slept, thus having to spend the following day with an oppressive odor.

It was a simple thing that she did but so illustrative of her new sensitivity and concern for others in response to God's care for her. She woke each man up at two in the morning and reminded him about the toilet.

I returned to the interview with Pastor Brown:

"Where do you find renewal for your personal faith. What gives you the energy and zeal to give your life in this way?"

"Well," he thoughtfully replied. "There is not much here to attract most pastors. The living conditions could be better, the salary's pretty small, there are not many social rewards such as in wealthier parishes, and the people are constantly in crisis. But I see each and every person as a child of God. I suffer with folks in their personal problems and they know it. I use suffering to point to the meaning of the gospel. These people cannot articulate their faith as members in better-educated parishes, but they can experience faith through my love for them and their own willingness to suffer for each other."

As Joe spoke, I recalled the scripture verse,

> Have this mind among yourselves, which is yours in Christ Jesus, who, though he was in the form of God, did not count equality with God a thing to be grasped, but emptied himself, taking the form of a servant, being born in the likeness of men. (Phil. 2:5-7)

I felt this attitude was what gave Joe the vitality to serve such a congregation.

We continued our conversation and I discovered more about his faithfulness to people Jesus might have called, "lost, least, and last."

"Preaching is among the most important things I do. For me, preaching is getting theology out of the head into the heart. Of course, people here do not usually respond with intellectual comments. Instead, the folks show me they understand by occasional acts of love and concern. One of the men kept caring for another who had a drug problem. When the abuser finally asked him why he was being assisted, his helper replied, 'because I've found a new life myself in my church, and I care for you.' Incidents like this remind me that the gospel is central to life's renewal.

"But I have other resources of inspiration. Besides seeing people changed by faith, I take part in a ministerial support group. We meet weekly to share our trials and victories. I am also surrounded by a number of faith-filled associates whose examples of caring for the dispossessed is a constant joy for me. I read a lot and I attend out-of-parish conferences which keep my perspective and religious insights alive. Of course, my family has been supportive, and I appreciate the concern for my ministry by the denomination. Finally, I want to say that my own personal prayer life is also a foundation for my love of God and love for the people."

I grappled with a summary of that which gives Joe Brown his vitality and joy for ministry, and concluded: "Those church members and others in that blighted neighborhood know that Joe loves them because of his faith. Such an example gives them hope and helps them share their crosses with others until they experience resurrection and a new life. This grace of God changes a hopeless church into a vital mission: an example of spiritual vitality.

Powers of the Spirit: Intervention

4. *The Spirit may be present when an indescribable power breaks in to a person's life to heal suffering or redirect purposes or emotions toward the will of God.*

Intervention—"Put up the Sword"

Several years ago I was fired from a job that meant a great deal to me. Because I wanted to do well, I arrived early to pray for a productive day and often stayed late to accomplish more than my boss had expected. Then one Friday afternoon I was dismissed without warning. Needless to say, I was angry, distraught, and confused.

Going to sleep that night was impossible. My mind was in such a turmoil. I felt the firing was unjust and unmerited. Aren't they all?

I began to plan for retaliation. I was not going to be treated as I had been. I had rights. I could appeal to influential friends to override my employer or I could cause a fuss and make things disagreeable for the department. Such ideas began to take deeper root as the silent night hours passed, but about three in the morning, I had a most unusual experience.

The mental picture of Christ reprimanding Peter appeared clearly before me! I seemed to be actually present during the arrest when Peter grabbed a sword in order to defend his Lord. I even thought I heard Christ tell Peter to put up the sword and not retaliate.

However I tried, I could not wish away that vision of Christ meeting his enemies with peace, even love. Every time I thought of my own retaliation, the example of Christ confronted me in such a forceful fashion that I felt my anger weakening.

Slowly and gradually my attitude turned around. Instead of wanting to demand my rights, I began to consider how I could make the best of the situation. The night hours wore on and soon it was dawn.

By 7 a.m. my mind had been completely changed. I was willing to think about returning to work. I even felt I wanted to prove that I could measure up to disappointment and grow from the experience.

When Monday came, I was again at my desk, ready for the few remaining weeks on my contract. I sat there thankful for the mysterious events of Friday night, which, over and above my own wishes, turned what could have been defeat into victory.

Of course, I often look back on that experience. Each time I do, I am more and more impressed with the dramatic change in my heart and mind. At the beginning I had been determined to get even for being fired. What strange force intervened and turned me completely around?

But that was not the only intervention that I experienced. You recall that I had founded much of that job on prayer. I had prayed at the beginning and at the end of each day. My joy in the work was infused with prayer. So, needless to say, when I was dismissed, I found it a terrible threat to my reliance on prayer.

If my earnestness in prayer had not graced my employment with integrity so as to influence my employer with my accomplishments, what was the use of praying? If my developing career could not be helpfully influenced by prayer, why should I pray? Did I really know how to pray?

I had found unexpected help in accepting and overcoming my loss of the job, but the loss of my confidence in prayer was another matter. It seemed as though an important foundation of my spiritual life had been taken away from me. Praying became filled with doubt and hesitancy. I turned away from prayer as one who was disenchanted with hope.

But in the midst of my mistrust in prayer, I experienced an ally I had taken for granted. Even though I faltered in prayer, I discovered my reliance upon God did not disappear. I may have lost the ability to talk with God, but I did not lose my conviction that God was present. Somehow my mouth had been stopped. My prayer life had been shut down. My yearning to place myself in God's care had been discouraged. In my head I turned away from prayer, but in my heart I knew God still cared.

Into my doubt about prayer came my awareness about the eternity of God!

Why are so many testimonials published that suggest prayer always brings results? Prayer does not always guarantee the saving activity of God. God is with us even when prayer is absent.

Cautions About Spiritual Growth

As I strive to open my life more and more to the presence of God and the will of my Creator, I keep several observations in mind.

One: Spiritual growth is not a matter of becoming better than another person. My real competition in life is not with my neighbor but with myself. I have little power over other people, even though I am called to share their burdens, instead, I am accountable for my own life. The question is not whether I become better than someone else but whether I become a better person than I was yesterday.

Two: I have found it helpful to remind myself that spiritual insight and power are not a matter of either education or intelligence. Although these backgrounds may be helpful, the Spirit is not so much a condition of mind as of soul. Spiritual life is not generated by reasoning but by faith. I need to keep in mind that, besides all the contributions of noted theologians and professors, the message of our Lord was given to a few unschooled fishermen, persons of extraordinary faith rather than scholastic training.

Three: Spiritual growth teaches that development may bring more pain than joy, at least at first. As my spiritual values become clearer, the choices between good and evil become much more intense. I find it increasingly hard to give up those habits which I know are questionable and that I have enjoyed so long. I know I should kill the sinful man within me, but I have difficulty doing so. The burning of self-will is not easy. The struggle seems to heat up more and more as I come closer to casting off old ways and turning to the new and untried. It almost seems as though the gate to heaven is attained by passing through the fires of hell.

Four: There is no method or system of any kind that will ever guarantee the presence of the Spirit. The best that any procedure can do is to make us more open to receiving the Spirit if and when it comes. For the Spirit is a gift. It cannot be earned. It may come to us in spite of who we are or what we have done. Nor do we ever know when it will come. The Spirit is unpredictable. Like the wind, it blows where it will.

Five: There is a danger that those who do experience the Spirit will conclude that such security and inner peace is a feeling to be cherished for itself. Such is not the case. Spiritual life is not an opportunity to withdraw from the world but rather to feel new energy and new love so that we can go out into the world. When the words "spiritual retreat" are used in religious circles, it means that a person retreats to go forward, marshals his or her talents to attack.

When Isaiah and Jesus received the Spirit, it was in order that they might go out to bind up the brokenhearted and set at liberty those who are oppressed. The presence of the Spirit calls us to the same concern for others today.

"Proverbs of the Spirit"

If the guilt of sin is agitating your mind,
    how can you recognize peace of soul?
As long as you keep on counting dollars and cents,
    you cannot count your real wealth.
If you go to bed with a promiscuous friend,
    you will be insensitive to the love of your wife.
If you have a storm within your own heart,
    how can you hear the needs of others?
If you confess on your knees at night,
    you will stand straighter during the day.
If you always put yourself first,
    why do you wonder that you understand love last?
If you have given much to the poor,
    you have wealthy-joy in your being.
If you have not experienced the anguish of suffering,
    you cannot recognize the cry of pain.
If your life is not grounded on God,
    how can you be moral in an immoral society?
If you have money in the bank,
    how can you fully understand those who are poor?
If you have not eaten with sinners,
    you will not know the joy of the saint.

And the Glory Forever and Ever

"Righteous Father,
The World hath not known Thee,
But I have known Thee
Joy, Joy, Joy, tears of Joy.
My God, wilt thou ever leave me?
Let me not be separated from Thee forever."

—Pascal, *Memorial* (A reference to his mystical experience. Found recorded on a piece of paper, inside of his coat, 1654)

"My Tattered Coat"

This page notes a high mileage mark on a long spiritual journey. The trip has been smooth and enjoyable as well as rough and unhappy. There have been many unexpected pleasures and a lot of unanticipated detours. As John Bunyan reported in Pilgrim's Progress, I, too, have known Sloughs of Despond and visions of the Celestial City. Like Bunyan, I have met a number of Worldly Wisemen and many Mr. Hopefuls.

As a minister I have traveled with Rev. Mr. Genuine and Rev. Mrs. Faithful; Rev. Mr. Misfit and Rev. Big Shot. In spite of a few who use the church for their own personal gain, I'm always inspired by the men and women I meet in ministry. They are pastors who care for those the world disdains, who help those the world neglects, and who serve those the world does not want. Yes, the integrity and faithful dedication of my peers are personal examples which challenge me to be a better disciple of Jesus Christ.

But I began to tell you about my spiritual journey. Let me say it has been hazardous. If you could see my clothes, especially my coat, you would see what I mean. It is tattered and torn.

It was not always that way. When I started out my coat was tailored and well-pressed. I imagine that when I walked down the street, there were those who said:

"There goes the pastor again. What a fine young man. What a spring in his step. How youthful he appears!"

Alas, they were looking at my clothes. It was my appearance and my status which impressed them. Most of my possible admirers did not know there was nothing inside, but I knew. I had a family heritage and some education, but I knew there was little else. I was ignorant about life, I was unacquainted with suffering, I may have been a Christian in my head, but I was not yet one in my heart. I really did not know my Lord.

But that was long ago. Now that once impressive coat is ripped and torn. In fact, it is so dilapidated that some of my friends don't recognize me or don't want to. They see my poor coat and pass by on the other side.

That's OK with me. I am not my coat and what they think they see is not me.

Even if others are embarrassed by the condition of my coat, I am not. I continue to wear it. It is a symbol of my experiences and of the many obstacles and troubles I have overcome. Some folks tell me that we create many of our own difficulties, that we don't understand and lack control of ourselves. Others say there is an Evil One on the road who purposefully misdirects anyone who picks him up.

I'm afraid I can't tell the difference between my self and that hitch-hiking adversary, but I feel powerfully influenced whenever I give him a ride. He has given me bad advice. He has led me

137

down useless byways and guided me to the low road. But when I experienced pain and sorrow, he was never around. So one of the purposes of this book is to expose this transient, in hopes that others will avoid his innumerable deceptions.

But I have forgotten about my coat. Years ago people were impressed about my appearance. I, too, was concerned about how I looked! But all that is changed. Now I care about who I am! I really don't need the coat any longer. I have little to cover up. I've told my story with so many of its frailties. I am who I am for all to see. I have no false position to protect. I am at peace. What is more, I have the time to walk any number of miles with anyone who needs a companion on their journey: I am someone who supports others in their dreams and helps them in their hopes.

So I'm ready to throw away my tattered coat. Instead of owning coats and things, I want to join a fellowship which is not held together by the clothes of status but by the bonds of openness and truthfulness.

I want to live with that great cloud of witnesses, men and women down through the ages, who have seen the same vision, been moved by the same Spirit, and suffered with the same Lord.

I want to join the Christian faith, which has outlasted the protective shells of so many nations. I want to serve the Master, who more than anyone else has given life it's fullest meaning.

I want to become more than I am through the power of the Holy Spirit, which has already emboldened me with a courage I do not fully comprehend but which, I believe, is the force that shapes the world and guides everyone toward the kingdom of God.

I want to spend my life with that cause which has freed people from their own self-destruction, empowered women to find their rightful place alongside men, repeatedly broken the bow of the aggressor, lifted up the stranger in the land, given equality to the lowly, and set the vision of justice and mercy before the world.

As I find this hope in the future, let me not forget the past. I have often disbelieved, I have doubted, and I have broken commandments. In short, I have been chastised by the presence of God. Indeed, I may have to go through it all again, for I'm still so imperfect. In fact, all of us must experience the continuing, cleansing chastisement of God; that is the badge of membership in the church and of growth in the Lord. However, it brings with it reconciliation as well as joy and security, which, unfortunately, the world does not understand.

Oh yes, my coat. I almost forgot about it. What shall I do with it? Who would want it?

The "hitch-hiker" will want it. He deals in clothing which covers hollow prestige and empty status. I'll give my coat to him. Once it was protection for my own emptiness. Now I have no need for such a covering because I have found my self, my faith and my Shepherd; they cover me. I have a Protector who is also a light to my path, a measuring rod to my faith, and a way of life to my future.

The world is filled with people in such coats as I wore. Those who, by faith, can cast them off, will walk instead in the shining coatless armor of God.

The Joy of Ministry

A young man whose mother wedded another minister in her second marriage observed, "Being the son of ten commandments is tough, but being the son of twenty commandments is tough enough!"

Even if there were fifty commandments, the spiritual life of a pastor would be filled with freedom, for we live not according to the law but by the direction of our conscience and our understanding of the will of God. Our responsibility to a congregation may be strained at times because we see the world as it ought to be, while church members see life as it is. But we have more freedom than is given to most people. The hours may be long, but the minister is boss of his or her own time, and we can regulate the degree of pressure from our duties. While everybody may expect us to do this or that, very few churches actually direct our schedules or even demand an accounting of our time. Hence, we live by the love of our work, rather than by regulations or laws. We are governed by what is inside rather than what is outside of us.

Artists may fill our days with beauty, and things may make all of our lives easier, but the most important aspects of life are mind and soul. Beauty is admired by all and materialism has its place, but there is nothing more valuable than a living person. Because this is the daily arena of our lives as pastors, we know we are dealing with the most important part of God's world. In comforting the sick, teaching the young, enabling adults to fulfill their lives, pardoning those who fall, and always preaching love and peace, we pastors know that our work is touched with the Spirit of Jesus Christ. Though we may differ in our individual loyalties to our Lord, we are all joyous in being part of the visible and invisible church of God. Like a mighty army we enthusiastically tread where the saints have trod.

The minister's role is not above frustration, rebuff, or even failure. We have enemies and those who put obstacles in our path. Still, we are moved by a vision. We live not for ourselves but for God, and we reply as did Nehemiah to those who would propose our defeat, "I am doing a great work and I cannot come down" (Neh. 6:3). In fact, we are in the employ of the Creator. Hence, we do not fear either our adversaries or the future. In spite of the circumstances of the day, we live for the city of God of tomorrow!

Amen

"I Have Seen My Salvation"

I have seen bombed-out populaces rebuild demolished cities; dry bones of despair coming to life again.

I see young men and women in their prime begin new churches in neighborhoods which all others have forsaken. And I know the vision of St. Paul planting new churches in Macedonia still lives.

I have seen nature overgrow deserted highways and broken monuments. And I know creation is stronger than death.

I have seen the evil dreams of dictators lost in the ongoing development of new nations. So I know the pharaohs cannot keep people in slavery.

I have seen men whose lives were caught in drug abuse saved by their acceptance of the gospel, like men who sat by the pool and were made whole again by faith in Christ.

I hear my peers preach courageous sermons of justice for the oppressed. And I know the spirit of Amos still moves among the people.

I see men and women find faith to face terminal illnesses. So I know the promise of Jesus is true, "Come unto me, and I will give you rest."

I know experienced Christian leaders who bring new hope to oppressed minorities. And I realize that Nehemiahs still rebuild.

I know of mothers who give birth in hope, even while they hear powerful politicians threaten humankind with nuclear suicide, even as Mary gave birth in the time of cruel Herod.

I see dilapidated store fronts in broken ghettos transformed into clean and painted buildings as Christians make places for worship and community education. So I know the word of the Lord continues to bring light into the darkness.

I experience the mystery of loving and being loved.

I know young men and women who dream of unselfish servanthood to Christ.

I have seen the martyrdom of prophets in my own time. I know that sacrifice gives the church new strength and power.

I know old women with crinkled faces who reflect not old age but peace, laughter, and joy because they are volunteers, helping others in Christ's name.

I see the word becoming the bread of life.

My own life has been reshaped into a maturity which I never expected through the caring Christian fellowship of my peers in ministry and of loving church members.

I see the possibility of my own salvation. So I pray to sit in the seat of Simeon, whose eyes saw God's salvation in the infant Jesus.

And if the power of salvation can touch me, one of a multitude of sinners, it can touch everyone.

I am part of the New Age, which has already begun.

I know nothing can hold back the dawn.

God reigns! The earth is the Lord's! Praise be to God!

Amen.

Notes

1. St. Augustine, *Confessions,* tr. F. J. Sheed, Sheed and Ward, 1942, p. 135.

2. John Bunyan, *Grace Abounding to the Chief of Sinners,* Chicago:Allenson, 1955, pp. 20, 28, 66.

3. By the late Henry Horner.

4. Evelyn Underhill, *The Life of the Spirit and the Life Today,* London:Methuen & Co., Ltd., 1922